PIPES
&
TOBACCO

The Book of

PIPES
&
TOBACCO

by Carl Ehwa, Jr.

Picture research by Marion Geisinger

A Ridge Press Book • Random House, New York

Editor-in-Chief: Jerry Mason
Editor: Adolph Suehsdorf
Art Director: Albert Squillace
Project Art Director: Harry Brocke
Associate Editor: Moira Duggan
Associate Editor: Barbara Hoffbeck
Associate Editor: Jean Walker
Art Associate: Mark Liebergall
Art Associate: David Namias
Art Production: Doris Mullane

Published in the United States by Random House, Inc.,
New York, and simultaneously in
Canada by Random House of Canada, Limited, Toronto.
Prepared and produced by The Ridge Press, Inc.

Library of Congress Cataloging in Publication Data
Ehwa, Carl.
    The book of pipes and tobacco.
    "A Ridge Press book."
    1. Tobacco-pipes.   2. Smoking.   I. Title.
GT3020.E47   1974   394.1'4   78-159341
ISBN 0-394-47000-1

Printed in Italy by Mondadori Editore, Verona.

For my grandfather, Dr. W. C. McClelland,
and my wife, Maria—
without her help there would be no book

Contents

Acknowledgments

I would like to express my gratitude to the following
people for their help while I was gathering information for this book:
Mr. Fred C. Diebel, Jr., master pipemaker and president of Diebel Tobacco;
Mr. Dave Ballard, master blender for the House of Edgeworth;
Mr. Aubrey Evelyn, private brands manager for the House of Edgeworth;
Mr. Paul Fischer, master pipemaker
and head of Paul Fischer Meerschaum Company.
I will always be in their debt.

Introduction

Transformation of choice tobacco leaf into a mixture that excites the palate is an art. No less an accomplishment is the skillful fashioning of beautiful pipes—from wood, gourd, or meerschaum. Pipe smoking is the appreciation of these arts. Smoking a pipe should be more than mere habit, more than simply satisfying a hunger. Fine tobaccos smoked in a worthy pipe stimulate the senses and calm the nerves.

Who can say what satisfactions man derives from smoking his favorite tobaccos or sampling excellent dishes, or even why being by a fire on a winter's day delights him as it does? One can say only that it is those small things that lend enjoyment to life, that refresh us and leave us ready to begin again.

The more knowledgeable and experienced the smoker, the better he is able to recognize excellence. To sharpen discriminating faculties and introduce the range of satisfaction to be had is the aim of this book. Even with the recent upsurge of interest in pipes, far too many smokers fail to appreciate pipe smoking for its full worth. Is this because of the pace of our lives? Perhaps, in part; but one can also point to the deficiency of information available about pipes and tobaccos. Both subjects need to be explored before full appreciation and enjoyment of pipe smoking is yours. Unfortunately, creative or constructive approaches to pipe smoking are scarce. Most of the literature available does not delineate the available products or the problems that may arise from improper selection or usage.

Also, the smoker, perhaps because he has been misled, too often lacks the patience and persistence needed to learn all the nuances of smoking. He gives up—in many cases just as he is on the verge of success.

Once the pipe smoker has formed a logical approach and put his knowledge into practice, so that the process of smoking becomes almost second nature, he is able to turn his full attention to savoring the flavors and aromas of superb tobaccos smoked in a comfortable, satisfying pipe.

May I offer my services as a guide, as provider of information and point of departure for your own thoughtful, productive explorations? May I share my discovery of the rewards of the pipe, one of the surviving reminders of gentler days when there was more time to savor each of life's pleasures?

Carl Ehwa, Jr.
Kansas City, Missouri

Part One
&
*The Remarkable Evolution
of
Smoking*

njoyment of tobacco seems such a well-established element of the civilized life that discovery of its relatively recent arrival in Europe astonishes many. Yet the earliest record of pipe smoking in England was written only in 1586. Who invented the tobacco pipe, then? And the leaves that men have literally died to smoke: Where did they come from? Botanists, economists, sociologists, archaeologists, and historians have striven to find out. Many of the answers elude us to this day.

From Persia, from Amerindian tribes, and from other far-flung peoples come myths and folk tales of how tobacco was introduced to grateful man. It is apparent testimony to man's appreciation of tobacco as, to quote Carlyle, "one of the divinest benefits that has ever come to the human race" that supernatural forces, the gods, are so often credited. A Russian legend has peasants learning to smoke and to plant the herb from Satan, who says, "Until now it was the mouth which ate; now it is the turn of the nose." Another legend explains how Lucifer acquired the plant: Ordered by God to take earth from the sea, the curious Lucifer put some in his mouth just as God said, "Let there be a world." As growth sprouted from this soil a terrified Lucifer obeyed the command to spit it out, and from this earth tobacco and hops grew.

In one tale, a band of Iroquois on an Ohio river were seeking to avenge the death of some brothers when a Voice urged them on to kill the murdering invaders and find a great blessing. And from the ashes of the bodies of those murderers grew a strange plant, a great gift, which the Voice instructed the Iroquois to use. From the first, tobacco has had divine properties.

Indians believed that tobacco smoke helped lift man's thoughts to the gods. We find a remarkable echo of this in Thomas Cooper's *Family Feud*, 1889: "How healthful are the private meditations of the true smoker! His plans

12

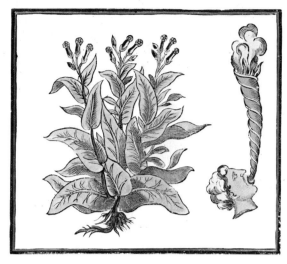

are properly matured and sagaciously practical ... yet he does not elaborate them, and dawdle with them, till all the fire has gone out of him. ...Nor are his thoughts all of the earth, earthy. The floating upward of that light wreath of vapour often reminds him of the ethereal aspirations and play of genius, or of the flight of a soul to its celestial home."

Mystery may surround the origin of tobacco—we cannot even be sure of the etymology of the word—but one thing is clear: Once its pleasures were revealed, it became a matter of developing the most efficient means of enjoying them. The pipe as it is known today has evolved through steady refinement of the practice in early times of inhalation of smoke from an open fire. We have Herodotus' account of a Scythian tribe: "They have a tree which bears the strangest produce [hemp]. When they are met together in companies they throw some of it upon the fire round which they are sitting, and presently, by the mere smell of the fumes which it gives out in burn-

ing, they grow drunk, as the Greeks do with wine." In his journal of 1681 an anonymous explorer in North America describes a boy smoking a two- or three-foot roll of tobacco and carrying it around a circle of men who greedily snuff the smoke he blows into their faces, seeming to bless themselves with the refreshment it gave. Among some Indians a clay pipe was built up from the ground, leading to descriptions of "earth-smoking," a practice also found, interestingly enough, in Africa as well as the grass steppes of Central Asia.

Tobacco in the New World

At the time of the first explorers, smoking in the New World was widespread. Each Indian group had some word signifying tobacco: in Brazil, *petum*; in Virginia, *uppowoc*; it was *quiecta* in the St. Lawrence region and *ziq* among Mayans; and in Trinidad, *vreit*. Natives also had found different ways to enjoy the weed. The Old World received the first report of tobacco from Christopher Columbus' chron-

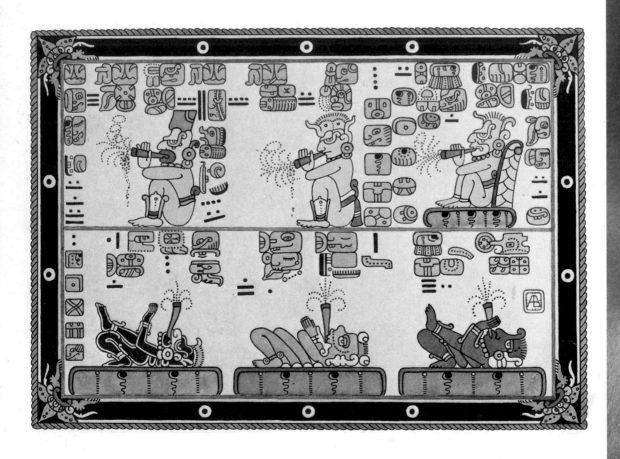

Illustration redrawn from pre-Columbian manuscript shows ancient Mayans of Central America puffing on conical cigars. Mayans believed smoking was "the eternal joy of the gods." Right: Prehistoric stone pipes fashioned by Indians of North America.

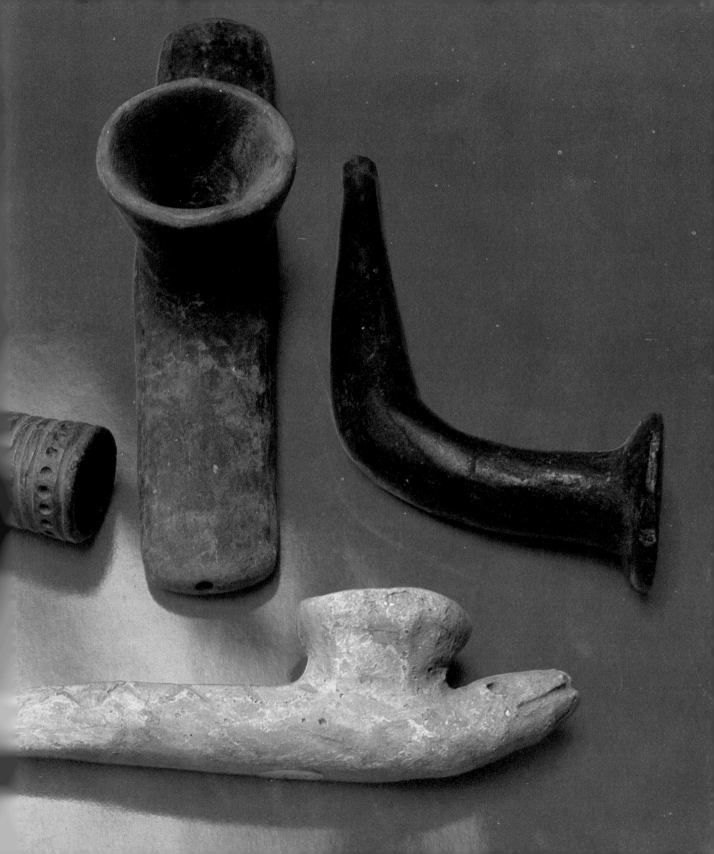

icler, Bishop Bartolomé de las Casas, who further described the Indians of Hispaniola as always having a "firebrand in their hand, and certain herbs for smoking. These were dry, and placed in a dry leaf, after the manner of those paper tubes which boys in Spain use at Whitsuntide." In 1499 Amerigo Vespucci saw Indians on Margarita Island off the Venezuelan coast chewing dry leaves. Friar Ramón Pané (whom Columbus charged with the task of reporting the ceremonies and customs of the natives) told of the ritualistic use of a powdered herb which was snuffed vigorously. The first cigarettes were seen in 1518 by Spanish explorers of Mexico, and Ponce de León in 1513 and Verrazano in 1524 supposedly saw pipe-smoking Indians in Florida.

The first smoking apparatus was probably of a straight, simple design. A bas-relief from the fifth century shows Mayans with tube pipes blowing smoke toward the sun to appease their gods, and we know that Aztecs used tubes of tortoise shell, silver, wood, and reed. But pipes were probably used much earlier, perhaps in the Bronze Age, when stone tubes may have been used on Crete.

Among Amerindians, chewing of tobacco must have preceded pipe smoking, pipes evolving as a kind of symbol of anthropological development from a hunting and gathering community to an agricultural one. The earliest written description of a tobacco pipe is found in Oviedo's *History of the Indies*, 1535. A two-pronged or Y-shaped tube was held to the nostrils, it reported. One stage in the pipe's evolution was observed by Walter Raleigh (or Ralegh, as he was originally named), who as a volunteer with French Hugenot explorers of Florida had ample opportunity to see and imitate the practice of smoking. In 1573 he wrote: "In these daies the taking in of the smoke of the Indian herbe called Tabaco, by an instrument formed like a little ladell, whereby it passeth from the mouth into the hed and stomach, is grettlie taken up...in England."

Perhaps the closest prototype of the European pipe comes from the Muskogee Indians of the southeastern United States. This group found that a tube pipe bent up at one end was better for carrying burning tobacco and allowed drawing more readily. From that design it was not far to the more familiar bowl. The refined pipe's ease of handling must have encouraged its manifold use in the religious, medical, political, and social areas of Indian life. It was even used by the Indians to mark time: An action would be described as having a duration of one pipe.

The widespread practice of smoking and the complicated native rituals recorded by the first explorers in America attest to a long-established habit. This supports the conclusion of most authorities that, along with corn, potatoes, and tomatoes, tobacco is native to the New World. Also relevant is the lack of mention of tobacco in the ancient works of Sanskrit

16

or Hebrew, on the monuments of Egypt or Chaldea, and in the reports of early travelers to the Orient. Not even Marco Polo, who took the greatest pains to include in his chronicles everything he observed, cites anything we could identify as tobacco.

This was instead left to Christopher Columbus. In March, 1493, the court of Spain was presented with alligator skins, screaming parrots, and reports of "gardens . . . the most beautiful I have ever seen in my life," of "sweet water in profusion," and of tobacco. That this solanaceous plant, the distant cousin of the garden pepper, petunia, and cucumber, should have been eventually the most rapidly and widely—though not royally—accepted of the New World's gifts to western man may have been largely due to the postmedieval European's lust for new tastes. This same desire, along with expanded trade made possible by growth of capital during the Renaissance, had spurred Columbus in his search for a new avenue to the much-sought spices of the Orient.

Several species of tobacco were being smoked at the time. In Mexico and the eastern United States and Canada, tribes had long cultivated the small-leaved *Nicotiana rustica*, which, though it was bitter and strong, was smoked in pipes. (It was evidently *N. rustica* which Jacques Cartier, who explored the St. Lawrence River in 1534-5, sampled. "We have tried this smoke; after taking some into our mouths it seemed like pepper it was so hot,"

Woodcuts of 1557 illustrate Brazilian natives' use of tobacco: Smoking a primitive cigar (top) and curing a sick man with smoke. Left: Pipe-smoking American Indian in 18th-century engraving has claws and almond-shaped eyes. N. tabacum *is more accurately drawn, though out of scale.*

19

he wrote.) In Central and South America the milder *Nicotiana tabacum* was being cultivated and smoked as cigars as well as in pipes. In addition, several species of wild tobacco which grew in the western portions of both continents were being smoked by natives. (Some of these species go unused today; others, which probably were collected and transported to Europe by early botanists, have been used scientifically throughout the world for nicotine and citric acid extraction, or merely to adorn gardens with their beautiful, flowering heads.)

Tobacco Arrives in Europe

All tobacco is called *Nicotiana* in honor of Jean Nicot, a French ambassador to Portugal, who presented *N. rustica* at the French court. Because of Nicot's charm and ability to exploit his product, he was credited with introducing tobacco in France, although the first packets had come there four years earlier, in 1556 or 1557. At that time, André Thevet had noted in Brazil what we call *N. tabacum* and carried it to France. But knowledge of Thevet's discovery did not reach the court of Henry II and so he never received proper recognition.

Today *N. rustica* still grows wild abundantly in the Western Hemisphere and some is grown in Russia, India, Western Europe, and Africa, though not for world trade. *N. tabacum*, which was the tobacco introduced to Spain, is the mother of all today's fine commercially grown tobaccos, and it was through

trade of the "Spanish leaf" that tobacco's popularity spread through Europe.

Among the Indians tobacco was an established medium of barter. A few years after the Mexican conquest in 1519, the missionary priest Bernardino de Sahagún, who was one of the first Europeans to distinguish the two major species of tobacco, noted the preparing and selling of leaves. About 1528 Cabeza de Vaca recounted how natives "give whatever they possess" for tobacco. Initially, Europeans overlooked the economic and recreational possibilities of tobacco; it was spices and gold that they sought.

Sailors were the first to acquire the tobacco habit they observed and it was sailors who spread the taste for tobacco, as they carried it from port to port in pigs' bladders. Tobacco, probably *N. rustica,* was introduced to Portugal by returning seamen during the first half of the sixteenth century. Several decades passed before tobacco's benefits and pleasures became the sensation of Europe, but the foundations of trade were being established. The Spanish and Portuguese, the first consumers of tobacco in the Old World, eventually became the envy of Europe as they developed their own plantations in America. Cortés had seen tobacco cultivation as an established agricultural art in Mexico in 1519, and soon thereafter Spanish planters had great success with the crop in Santo Domingo. (By 1580 good tobacco was being grown on a large scale by Spaniards in Trinidad, Cuba, and Venezuela.) Tobacco was being cultivated in the Portuguese colony of São Vicente, Brazil, in 1534, and sixteen Portuguese settlements along the Brazilian coast were exporting tobacco to Lisbon in 1548. As the Portuguese continued their explorations they disseminated knowledge and appreciation of tobacco. They were the ones to bring tobacco to the Arabs, whose word for it was "Bortugal."

English, French, and Dutch mariners developed a taste for tobacco as a result of raids on Spanish ships and settlements where the booty included this herb. Dutch and Portuguese traders almost simultaneously introduced the pleasurable habit to seaports in Persia, Indo-China, and Java. It is difficult to believe that the Europeans had anything new to teach the long-cultured people of China and Japan, but the Portuguese, powerful in the Indian seas, knew of reed and cane pipes from Brazil and were responsible for introducing the prototype of Far Eastern pipes. Tobacco smoking quickly became firmly entrenched in that part of the world and Asian craftsmen took the making of pipes for their own art. A wonderful variety of pipes emerged, including pipes of jade from the Yarkand River in Asia and delicately carved pipes from Korea and China that were remarkable for their tiny bowls (appropriate for the potent mixtures of tobacco and opium favored in the Orient).

By the early seventeenth century, tobacco was well known to all continents except Australia, its course making a kind of full circle as the pipe introduced to the Chinese by sixteenth-century Europeans was brought to the Eskimos, who in turn carried it down to American Indians of the Northwest, with local tradition and art always adapting the basic pipe. Entire legends were carved on the sides of Eskimo pipes; Lapps fashioned a one-piece pipe out of a walrus tooth; fishing peoples, whether Cornish or Nova Scotian, made pipes from lobster and crab claws; and in Szechwan province of China gracefully bent bamboo was used, while willow branches served similarly for the Eskimos. Europeans were responsible for the spread of the enjoyment of tobacco within South America as well; there is no evidence that natives in Bolivia, Peru, Chile, and the area south of Brazil used it before the arrival of European explorers.

As the enjoyable aspects of smoking were being quietly diffused by mariners, sixteenth-century New World explorers discovered more and more the part tobacco played in the lives of the Indians. It was a divine gift worthy of a place in Indian treaty councils and social intercourse alike. Smoke blown over the heads of warriors gave them strength in battle. Pipe magic among certain tribes included a ritual similar to the making of an effigy or voodoo. The chief would take a pipe cleaning stick, scrape ash on the ground three times,

*Views of the New World
executed by Flemish engraver in 1590
show "Columbus at Hispaniola"
(top) and "The Town of Secota" (r.),
an Indian village with
square plot of N. rustica tobacco
(marked E, at top). Effigy
pipes (l.) are from Indian burial mounds,
date between A.D. 900 and 1500.
Far left: Sketch of N. rustica in flower.*

24

Chief of a South American Indian
tribe smokes a long, straight pipe during
ceremonial petum, or tobacco dance, while
Europeans (r.) prepare to dine and member
of ship's company tootles his bagpipes.
Engraving was published in 1621.

and end the intonations of his curse on his enemy with "This for the crown of his head." Usually, however, the pipe symbolized agreement and friendship, and many an early explorer relaxed when he saw the chief take up his *calumet*, the ceremonial peace pipe.

One of the reasons for Europe's initially slow adoption of smoking tobacco was its intellectual climate; a prevailing puritanical attitude frowned on the pagan and deemed smoking for pleasure sinful. Smoking plants and herbs other than tobacco had been prescribed for "windy griefs of the breast" by European physicians since the Middle Ages. But tobacco's emergence as a universal cure-all in the mid-1500s acted as a catalyst, increasing its acceptance and popularity. Damiâo de Goes, archibishop to the Portuguese king, sanctioned the imported herb as "holy" and having miraculous power.

Las Casas early recognized tobacco's use in combating fatigue. In 1564, John Sparke, who accompanied John Hawkins to Florida, described a pipe without being able to name it and recorded that the "Floridians have a kind of herbe dried . . . which smoke satisfieth their hunger and therewith they have four or five days without meate or drinke, and this all the Frenchmen used for this purpose." Jean Nicot wrote to the Cardinal of Lorraine on the 26th of April, 1560, "I have got hold of a frightfully interesting Indian herb, which heals boils and

25

running sores, which up to now seemed incurable. . . .'' Tobacco was hailed as an aid against plague, useful in time of headache or stomach cramps, and, at one time or another, a remedy for abscesses, arthritis, bleeding, burns, cancer, deafness, dropsy, halitosis, hernia, lethargy, mania, pneumonia, syphilis, whooping cough, and warts, to mention only a few. Historical rosters of its ill effects are far shorter. All sorts of experiments were conducted. Oint-ments and syrups were made of tobacco, people gargled and chewed it, rubbed it on their skin, used it as an eye wash, and blew it into each others' intestines with specially designed bellows. (Reportedly such a ''tobacco enema'' resuscitated a young woman found drowned in a Dutch canal.) A 1622 medical dissertation cited approximately one hundred different prescriptions using tobacco. Tobacco was not only for the sick; in the sixteenth and seven-

From top l.: Totemic slate pipe, probably Haida Indian, from Queen Charlotte Island, "cat" pipe from the Upper Nile, Basuto pipe (with horse figure) from South Africa, Lapland pipe of carved reindeer horn, and two catlinite bowls of Plains Indian pipes flanking an Eskimo tusk pipe decorated with whaling scenes.

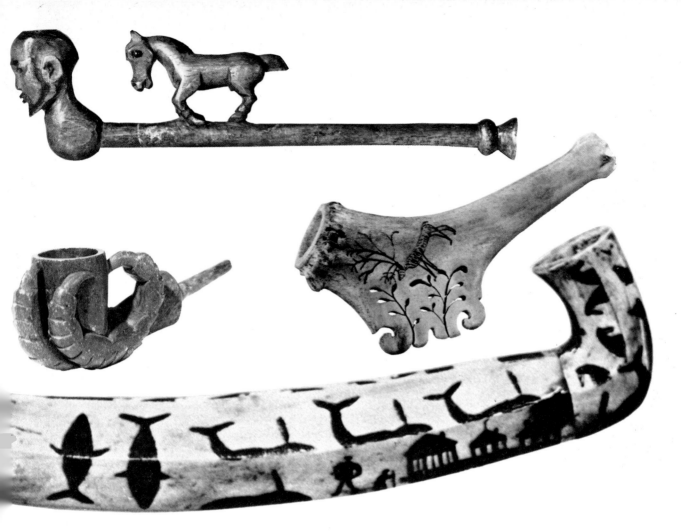

teenth centuries it was employed in love potions and mixtures for the preservation of perennial youth.

Soon the herb which had been of interest only to botanists in Europe was in great demand, thereby profoundly affecting world trade, not to mention the history of North America. There was virtually no tobacco grown in Europe; the first record of the plant as part of a garden there dates back only to 1554, in Belgium. As limited producer and enormous consumer, the Low Countries have from the start been an important part of the tobacco market. Holland took to tobacco before the British—probably as early as 1550—and for a century, it consumed more per capita than England or Germany.

As far as we know the first tobacco arrived in England directly from the New World with John Hawkins in September, 1565.

A botanical work published in 1570 by Doctors Pena and L'Obeh records: "You see many sailors, and all those who come back from America, carrying little funnels made from a palm leaf or a reed, in the extreme end of which they insert the rolled and powdered leaves of this plant." It remained to Sir Walter Raleigh, that most famous tobacco promoter, to recognize and further enjoyment of the "witching weed" in the British Isles. Commissioned by Raleigh as a historian and sur-

veyor in America, Thomas Hariot returned in 1586 with two related plants, tobacco and potato, and notes for a manuscript, "A briefe and true report of the new found land of Virginia: of the commodities there found and to be raised, as well marchantable, as others for victuall, building and other necessarie uses for those that are and shall be the planters there. . . ."

Before that information could even be published, Raleigh planted a patch of to-

Calumets, or peace pipes, of American Plains Indians had bowls of red catlinite, a clay stone from sacred quarry in Minnesota. Carved wooden stems were decorated with animal effigies, beads, or feathers, depending on pipe's ceremonial use.

bacco in Ireland, where he was governor of Kilcolgan. He enthusiastically adopted and publicized smoking. His eminence as a national hero helped his cause, and England quickly made up the time it had lost. Raleigh had one of his great rooms made into a "tabagerie" where he encouraged friends to accustom themselves to the correct techniques of pipe smoking. Raleigh's pipe accompanied him always, even to the scaffold.

A pipe and proficiency in its use became standard equipment for the beaux of London. Newcomers to town heard they should visit the middle aisle of St. Paul's Cathedral—not to sightsee or pray but to examine the placards of the smoking instructors who advertised their specialties there. Any true gallant wanted to be proficient in the various smoking tricks of the day, which included "the Whiffe," "the Ring," "the Gulpe," "the Retention," and those with outlandish designations, such as "the Cuban Ebolition" (ebullition, actually, a rather agitated exhalation of smoke), "the Euripus" (a rapid inhalation and exhalation of smoke in a rhythm that apparently suggested a channel of water known to the ancients for its violent flux), or "Receit Reciprocall" (probably making smoke rings of increasing or decreasing size). It was preoccupation with such dandified pursuits that Ben Jonson satirized in *Every Man in His Humour*. We should not be too quick to scoff at these follies. Recent times have seen international smoking competitions from Copenhagen to Buenos Aires, preceded by earnest training sessions at local clubs and followed by prize awards for such feats as the slowest smoke (3.3 grams of Burley in a clean pipe, with only two matches allowed—one German managed forty-three minutes, eleven seconds!).

Does history record any other custom spreading with such rapidity? The first mention of English clay pipes, for example, was made in 1598, and by 1615 a visitor to the Bear Garden in Southwark could remark "tobacco shops are now as ordinary as taverns and tap-houses." The "sovereigne Herbe" has since seen some stormy times—there has never seemed to be a neutral zone in the debate—but the early seventeenth century was clearly ripe for the spread of smoking. Smoking tobacco for medical purposes tapered off (although the therapeutic value of smoking was endorsed until the nineteenth century), but smoking as a social habit progressed, despite the opposition of James I of England and supreme rulers elsewhere. The extent of the acceptance and adoption of tobacco can be measured in many different ways. One dramatic indication was the strength of the defiance to royal opposition to smoking—sometimes to the point of risking death. It was when smoking was no longer simply sober recreation but extremely fashionable that it met ridicule, censure, and imperial decree.

The serious attack on smokers began

with the pamphlet "Work for Chimny-Sweepers," which was written under a pseudonym. The first public debate on tobacco, clearly a staged affair, was held at Oxford in 1605. James I set up a pipemakers' guild in London in an attempt at greater supervision of the detested industry and, when his subjects refused to heed his counsel, he moved to increase the duty on tobacco 4000 percent—the one move which did have some impact.

James' actions had parallels among his contemporaries elsewhere. Czar Michael of Russia believed smoking and sniffing were deadly sins, prompting the most severe punishment. First offenders had their noses slit, recurrent sinners were put to death or deported to Siberia. Turkish and Persian smokers caught in the act were led through the streets with pipes thrust through their noses—if they weren't beheaded. Still, in Turkey the praises of tobacco were sung loud and clear as it was esteemed one of the four cushions of the "couch of pleasure." In China, tobacco was proclaimed by the people the soul-reviving "herb of love" —while their ruler proclaimed it subversive of the national interest. Since no threat of punishment seemed to deter Chinese smokers, it was decreed that foreigners found importing tobacco would be decapitated. Among possible justifications for such drastic decrees could be numbered a fear of fire or ill health, or concern, especially in the Far East, that the vital rice crop would be neglected for cultivation of

the new herb. (Obsession with tobacco growing did become a problem in the colony of Virginia.) We can also understand Pope Urban VIII, who was driven in 1642 to issue a bull forbidding the practice of priests and clerks smoking while celebrating mass. But often condemnation arose from mere distrust of alien customs and from ignorance, with more than one surviving document of censure citing those ancient tales of the demonic origins of tobacco.

Smoking withstood all tests and flourished. Pipemakers were hard pressed to keep up with the demand for clays, which were extremely breakable. Many a student at Leyden would buy a half basket of the long pipes at a time (one basket held one hundred and sixty pipes). As demand for tobacco grew and supply was uncertain, prices fluctuated violently. In 1599 Cuban tobacco sold for as much as four pounds, ten shillings a pound in London. Because Spain had developed her plantations in the New World so early, she monopolized the market. Englishmen turned westward as the seventeenth century dawned to seek relief from the dominance of Spain as their tobacconist.

Tobacco and the Colonies

The Chesapeake colonies could truly be said to be "founded upon smoak" as English adventurers and entrepreneurs set out to develop colonial sources of tobacco. A leader among

Tomahawk trade pipes (top) for which Indians bartered away land and furs. Stems often were highly decorated, in manner of beribboned Chippewa pipe. Right: Trapper smokes a peace pipe in Alfred J. Miller's "Indian Hospitality."

such men was John Rolfe, himself a confirmed smoker before he voyaged to Jamestown. Led by Rolfe, the original settlers of Jamestown intended to produce merchantable tobacco, but they found the tobacco grown by the Indians along the James and other rivers in Tidewater Virginia too harsh. By 1612, Rolfe had procured Spanish seed (*N. tabacum*) through a shipmaster voyaging to Trinidad, thus bringing it north of the Caribbean area for the first time. The next year the first leaves reached England. In 1614 seven thousand shops in London sold tobacco and by 1618 the Virginia Company had shipped the first 20,000 pounds of its crossbred, "sweet-smelling" tobacco to England in successful competition with Spain. The Spanish monopoly—including the privilege of imposing exorbitant prices on smokers in other countries—had been broken. Within a decade, Virginia was exporting 500,000 pounds of tobacco annually.

This was in spite of James I, who, besides denouncing tobacco in a book, levied great duties on it and restricted the Virginia Company's production. Americans, however, neither then nor later put the whims of government before good business. Tobacco dominated the lives of the Virginians. Jamestown was transformed through its success from the pesthole, plagued with incompetent leaders and shortsighted fortune-hunters, which Thomas Dale had been sent to reorganize in 1611. Virginians themselves became industri-

ous and so deeply involved with tobacco that at one time in the very early days of the colony Rolfe expressed serious concern over the lack of attention given to the growing of staple foods. Laws soon had to be written to control the tobacco fever. One limited colonists to one thousand plants (by 1629 it was changed to three thousand). As a matter of fact, reading the laws of the Virginia Colony, one finds no product receiving so much attention as tobacco. It was a good example of the system of colonial specialization which eventually made England the wealthiest nation on earth. In a 1617 report, Captain John Smith wrote that he "found but five or six houses, the Church down, the 16 palisades broken, the bridge in pieces, the well of fresh water spoiled . . . [because] the colony was dispersed all about, planting tobacco."

It is not hard to understand why the colonists treated tobacco as they did—growing it in the streets, in houses, anywhere a plant could be squeezed in. Wives as well as servants were bought with the leaf. In 1619 the first cargo of Negro slaves deposited in Virginia by the Dutch was paid for with tobacco. Two years later transportation charges for "mail order brides" from England came to one hundred and twenty pounds "best leaf" tobacco per wife. Clergy were paid in tobacco and did not seem to mind association with a product some of their forebears had attacked.

Despite James' impositions, more

32

Beginnings of tobacco industry in America. Top: Colonial Tidewater planter oversees slaves as they pack hogsheads bound for England. Right: Earliest illustration of a tobacco factory, c. 1667-1671, shows process of manufacturing roll, or "rope," tobacco.

p. 419

FACTORY-YARD

1. Petum [Tobacco] -house.	4. Negro who rolls it.	8. The Press.	12. The kitchen
2. Negro who tears the tobacco apart.	5. Negro who scrapes the manioc [cassava]	9. Negress sifting the flour.	13. Cassava drying.
3. Negro who twists it.	6. Mill to grind the manioc.	10. Negress who cooks the cassava.	14. Corozo-tree.
	7. Ancient method of grinding the manioc.	11. The house of the master.	

The Earliest Known Illustration Showing An American Tobacco-Factory. From the HISTOIRE GENERALE DES ANTILLES, by Father Jean Baptiste Du Tertre, Paris, 1667-1671.

Englishmen than ever took up smoking. Ironically, because of his high tariffs, James was one of the first to profit greatly from the import of tobacco. In 1621 the House of Commons passed an act providing a system of preferential tariffs for tobacco and the fostering of colonial enterprise. The succeeding phases of governmental limitation of the amount of Spanish tobacco imported, in return for the colonists' promise to ship only to England, led to one of the most complicated periods in English commercial history.

There were years of tension between Virginia planters and English merchants when inferior and adulterated tobacco, distorted prices, and highly organized smuggling were common. The prohibition of 1673 against intercolonial trade led to Culpeper's Rebellion. Although limited to the Albemarle area of Virginia, it was a significant preview of rebellions to come. The "Rable" demanded from their new assembly the right "absolutely to insist upon a free trade to transport their tobacco where they pleased."

The effects of tobacco, America's first industry, on her political, economic, and social life—on her very composition—were profound and diverse. Production of tobacco guaranteed the permanence of the Virginia Colony and it was the cause of the first strains between the colonies and the mother country. As the size of the crop produced became the determining factor in a planter's success, the 100-acre farm

34   *"Raleigh's First Pipe in England"*
is a 19th-century caricature based on the
legend that a startled servant,
unaware of smoking and believing his master
ablaze, doused Sir Walter with water.
Pipe resembles that on page 24.

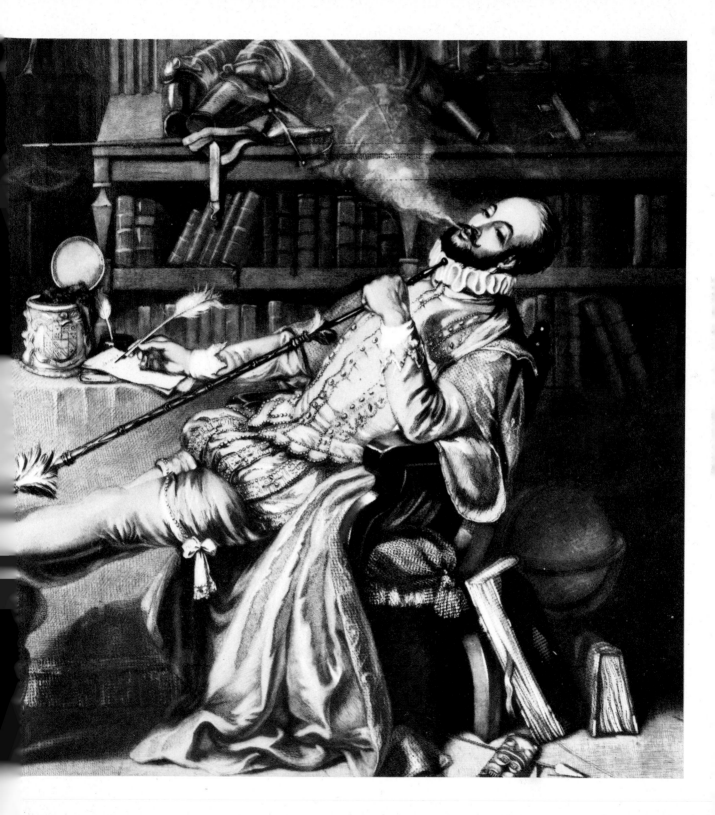

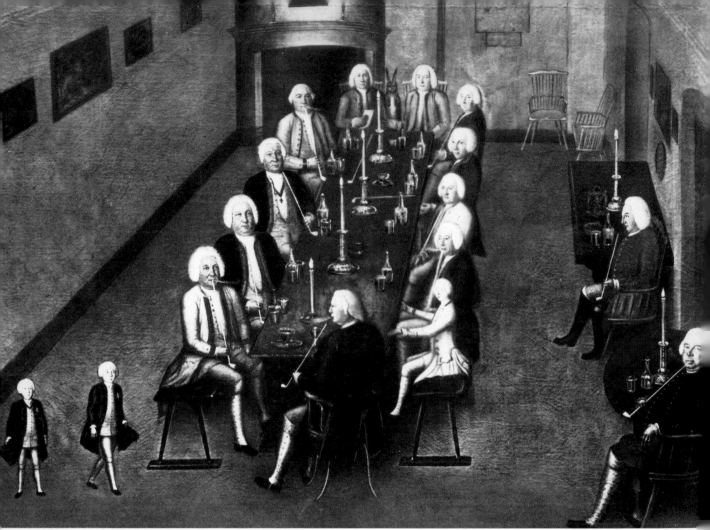

36

run by free citizenry became unfeasible, and so tobacco fostered the development of the plantation system and helped create the new South.

Planters, energetic men made wealthy by dint of their own labor, created their own aristocracy. Tobacco thus nurtured America's first families, the Byrds, Randolphs, and Harrisons, and colonial leaders such as George Washington and Thomas Jefferson. Cultivation of tobacco exhausts the soil after three years and as new land was needed, tobacco led to western expansion. The need for free access to seaports from those new western growing areas in turn led to support of the Louisiana Purchase. The War of 1812 was supported largely out of irritation at British interference with shipment of planters' staples; indeed, diplomacy for decades following the Revolutionary War was often directly influenced by concerns for the protection of tobacco interests.

A Social Habit Is Established

In England fifty years after the death of James, after-dinner smokes were enjoyed by women as well as men, and children carried a filled pipe to school, where the master conducted lessons in its use. To smoke, many believed, was necessary for good health. "Without tobacco one cannot live in England—it dissipates the evil humors of the brain," a French visitor to England noted. As a small irony of history, James I was the ancestor of Friedrich Wilhelm I, the smoking king of Prussia, who founded the famous Tabaks-Collegium, which became a political institution. In Carlyle's description of Hanoverian George I's smoking room, we get a sense of a high-ceilinged lounge, peopled by "contented saturnine human figures, a dozen or so of them, sitting round a large long table. . . . Perfect equality is to be the rule, no rising or notice taken, when anybody enters or leaves. Let the entering man take his place and pipe, without obligatory remarks; if he cannot smoke, which is Seckendorf's case for instance, let him at least affect to do so, and not ruffle the established stream of things."

Almost universally, smoking became a sign of fellowship, reminiscent of that first friendly offering of tobacco by the Arawak Indians Columbus encountered at San Salvador. It had been a common sign of amity for all early Americans and was to be the one example of Indian etiquette which western man adopted.

Around the first decade of the eighteenth century, one Peter Burmann recorded established European etiquette for our enlightenment: "It is not enough to fill a pipe and put it to the mouth and set fire to it, for even the country bumpkin knows as much. It is only correct to hold it dextrously with the left hand, have the right hand provided with a stopper, impress the onlookers with majestic mien, sit in the proper attitude on the chair,

Companionable clays of the 18th century: "Tobacco Parliament" of Friedrich Wilhelm I, Prussia's "Smoking King," sits for portrait with fragile, long-stemmed clays. Friedrich reputedly indulged in as many as thirty-two pipesful of tobacco each evening. Below: An English smoking club.

and finally, to take enough time for each pipe and not treat with hasty irreverence this heavenly food." Then it was accepted that a man's quality—his personality, life style, sensibilities, his very thoughts—was revealed in the way he held a pipe between the lips or knocked out ashes. England's Foreign Secretary Lord Clarendon purportedly said, "Diplomacy is entirely a question of the weed. I can always settle a quarrel if I know beforehand whether the plenipotentiary smokes Cavendish, Latakia, or Shag."

Pipe smoking became so enmeshed with daily life that Italian Queen Margherita in the last half of the nineteenth century could not imagine a household functioning smoothly without this civilizing pleasure. She said she would be able to forgive any conceivable fault in a husband save one, and that would be his being a nonsmoker, for the pipe would soothe the most ferocious of bad tempers.

Since the introduction of the pipe to western man, literature, journals, and art have been filled with testimony to its contribution to his happiness. From one century to another the comments parallel each other to a remarkable extent. A nineteenth-century Englishman wandering through a South American forest wrote, "Blessed be the man who invented smoking, the soother and comforter of a troubled spirit, allayer of angry passions, a comfort under loss of breakfast, and to the roamer in desolate places, the solitary wayfarer

Fashions in Tobacco: Boulevardiers by Daumier (top) are puffed up with cigar smoke and self-importance, while demoiselles by Boilly daintily sniff snuff. Right: Goya's majo (seated, l.) smokes a papelito in "La Cometa" (1776-1778)—the first cigarette to appear in a painting.

through life, serving for wife, children and friends." A Japanese author said it "is a companion in solitude; it is a store-house for reflection and gives time for the fumes of wrath to disperse." For Thackeray, "The pipe draws wisdom from the lips of the philosopher, and shuts up the mouth of the foolish."

The poetry which has tobacco and the pipe as themes does indeed range from the sublime to the ridiculous. The first full poem in English was Sir John Beaumont's 1602 work, *The Metamorphosis of Tabacco*, and an early piece of literature which gives the pleasures of tobacco due praise is Spenser's *Faerie Queene*—there again we read of "divine tobacco." But the most quoted and quotable of the English poems is Charles Lamb's sad "Farewell to Tobacco," 1805. Lamb, the man who made the half-jesting wish that he draw his last breath through a pipe and exhale it in a pun, actually could not bring himself to part with his pipe until a quarter of a century following his famous farewell. When asked how he had become such a prodigious smoker, he replied, "I toiled after it, Sir, as some men toil after virtue." For Molière, tobacco "is the passion of honest men and he who lives without tobacco is not worthy of living." There are other works, like Byron's "The Island," with its "Sublime Tobacco . . . Divine in hookahs, glorious in a pipe . . ." but most fascinating of all are the lesser-known pieces, the endless epics in verse as published in nineteenth-

century France in *Almanach des Fumeurs*, in publications like "Tobacco Talk and Smokers' Gossip, An Amusing Miscellany of Fact and Anecdote relating to the Great Plant," or the pamphlets put out by London tobacco processors and distributors. Printed there were playlets, anecdotes, curiosa of history, and practical advice, along with songs and odes. One, published in the February, 1757, issue of *Gentleman's Magazine*, opens:

"Tube, I love thee as my life;
By thee I mean to choose a wife
Tube, thy color let me find,
In her skin, and in her mind."

Memoirs and historical accounts offer hosts of examples of what tobacco—the pleasures of the pipe especially elicited poetry and reflection—meant to the smoker. Take a sidelight on the Battle of Viemeyro, in Portugal, August 21, 1808. An old cavalier, when finally rescued, gasped out these first words: *"Ils m'ont bien donné des coups de sabre, mais ils ne m'ont pas dépipé."* (They slashed me many times with their sabers but I never lost my pipe.)

The role pipes have played in art is a subject in itself. The pipe is there explicitly, as in the commentary it made on the self-consciousness of the Dutch burgher of the seventeenth century. Some art historians even find that the classical art of the Renaissance stands as the art of nonsmokers, whereas the following Baroque period reflects a dynamism, coupled with an inner harmony, a feeling of expansiveness and space, which they attribute to tobacco-smoking artists.

As artistic subject and inspiration, well-praised personal pleasure, and a force in politics and economics, enjoyment of tobacco has clearly withstood the challenges of time. Men have died to smoke—or at least fought for the right, as the Haarlem tobacco riots of 1690 or the March, 1848, revolution in Berlin attest. Smokers have opposed the reformers each century has produced—such as the American antitobacco societies of the 1800s and the admonishments of clergymen, physicians, educators, and speakers ranging from P. T. Barnum to Horace Greeley, who depicted the cigar as "a fire at one end and a fool at the other."

Most remarkable is the survival and current resurgence of popularity enjoyed by man's first smoking implement, the pipe.

At the close of the seventeenth century, snuff arrived from the French aristocracy to delight London's social elite and help them escape temporarily the foul odors of garbage-choked alleys. All manner of paraphernalia was invented for the elegant snuffer, books on snuff etiquette were read avidly, and this new pleasure supplanted the pipe until it became gauche to the style-conscious. The cigar remained a novelty outside of Spain and Portugal until English and French soldiers mingled with those from the Iberian Peninsula during the Napoleonic Wars. The expense kept ci-gars the indulgence of the wealthy and aristocratic from 1815 to 1825, but cigars did bring about a renascence of smoking as opposed to sniffing, and by the 1870s they were popular in the United States, nudging aside chewing.

Tobacco was a standard ration in the United States Navy during the Civil War years and it was issued to Confederate enlisted men by an act of the Confederate Congress. The United States was soon to have a dominant position in the next development for smokers: the cigarette. Not really a modern phenomenon, it had spread quietly eastward from its origin among Mexican Indians, through Spain, to Turkey and Russia. Brought west by soldiers returning from the Crimean War, the "pepelet," or cigarette, first caught on in England. Its popularity increased phenomenally at the end of the nineteenth century. It was a more convenient, cheaper smoke, and a symbol for the new tempo of the times, which saw the industrial revolution fostering a desire for immediate pleasures. Cigar manufacturers felt the bite of the cigarette industry and began advertising campaigns claiming that cigarette paper was made by Chinese lepers, that opium and morphine were mixed with cigarette tobaccos, that the paper contained arsenic. Smokers sought refuge from the fears these rumors fostered by smoking more cigarettes. Now the history of smoking seems to have come full circle as smokers discover anew the calming effects of a well-cared for pipe.

Part Two
The
Amiable Pipe

For nearly two centuries briar and meerschaum pipes have dominated the quality pipe-making industry to such an extent, and have proved so excellent in every way, that one can scarcely imagine they weren't used from the beginning. Yet until the middle of the nineteenth century, clay and porcelain pipes were the only kinds produced in any quantity.

Clay and Porcelain Pipes

It is unfortunate that the popularity of clay pipes has steadily declined, for, despite some drawbacks, they lend a very satisfying, earthy taste to tobaccos. By smoking these pipes, one can get an idea of what early smokers experienced. Today's clay pipes are virtually identical in both materials and methods of manufacture to those of two hundred years ago; actually, tobaccos have changed more than clay pipes.

To make this type of pipe, clay is ground in a mill and mixed with water until it has a smooth, workable texture. The molder rolls a lump of the prepared clay into a long stem and shapes a cone-like blob at one end, creating a form which will fit the final mold. Next, the caster takes the crudely shaped piece and runs a wire through the shank. Leaving the wire in place, he puts the pipe-in-progress into a halved mold with holes at each end and, using a hand press, forces the mold tightly shut. When the excess clay is forced out, a reaming device is pushed into the large end of the mold to form the inner bowl of the pipe. The pipe is removed from the mold and allowed to dry for several days. Then the seams created by the mold are scraped off and the pipe is ready for baking.

The wire is removed from the stem and the pipe put in a crock which is placed in an oven for about twenty-four hours, until the grayish clay becomes white. After the baking process, better manufacturers polish their pipes, generally with a wool cloth, and glaze

44

Preceding pages: William Harnett's "The Social Club" is a still life of familiar friends—briars, meerschaums, clays, cherry-wood stems, and bone bits— painted with extraordinary fidelity. Right: 19th-century British trade card.

the tips of the stems to keep them from sticking to smokers' lips.

Holland comes to the minds of most people when clay pipes are mentioned and rightly so, for the Dutch eventually became the leading producers. However, the English originated the refined form of clay pipe that began the pipemaking industry. Europeans began to take smoking seriously in the 1500s and pipe smokers quickly grew in numbers. This was particularly true in England, where it was natural to follow the example of the New World Indians by using clay for pipes, for clay was plentiful and already being used in fine forms by English manufacturers. Contemporary engravings often depict clay pipes being smoked in coffeehouses, pubs, even in churches. A long version of the clay pipe was dubbed the churchwarden.

By the early 1600s, England was a major producer of clay pipes, but with the death of Queen Elizabeth and the succession of priggish James Stuart, the royal view of to-

bacco changed. James's distaste was voiced in the most extreme way. In *Counter-blaste to Tobacco*, 1604, he said it was a "custom loathsome to the eye,...harmfull to the braine, dangerous to the lungs, and in the black stinking fume thereof, nearest resembling the horrible Stigian smoke in the pit that is bottomlesse." Needless to say, life became miserable for those who favored or trafficked in tobacco. But pipemakers did not take the king's abuses quietly. When Sir Walter Raleigh, that avid and persistent pipe smoker, was charged with treason and executed, English pipemakers began to champion their hero posthumously with pipes that had his effigy molded into the bowls. King James was furious and in 1620, after many unheeded warnings of the consequences of such defiance, set up a pipemakers' guild in London and made any practice of the trade outside the guild unlawful. Pipemakers began leaving the country in great numbers for Holland, and the Dutch and English-turned-Dutch began to control the clay-pipe industry.

45

With clays costing only a penny a gross in
17th-century Holland, even peasants could afford the
pleasures of smoking, as shown in Hendrik
Sorgh's convivial scene, "The Merrymakers." Above:
English clays, c. 1800, metal pipe cases, and
engraved Dutch tobacco boxes of late 18th century.

Thereafter, clay pipes changed very little as far as shape was concerned. All pipe-makers produced short, medium, and long-stemmed models. It was the art work molded into the bowls and stems in relief—mythological characters and beautiful designs of all types—along with heel, or bowl, marks—such as crowns or roses—which were early trademarks. In the Dutch city of Gouda, which gained preeminence for the quantity and quality of its clay pipes, approximately five hundred marks were registered in the year 1660.

In addition to pipes, beautiful hand-made items, the artistry of which has never been matched in modern times, were created to aid and complement the stylish smoker. At the same time they often reflected his occupation, religious feelings, or political views. Wood-carvers designed intricate hinged cases, often adorned with hand-painted story-telling scenes, and racks in which to rest pipes. Metal craftsmen produced fancy tobacco boxes engraved with Biblical themes, puzzles, poems, and songs; flint-and-steel cases; pipe tools; and braziers in which smoldering fuel such as peat was kept for lighting pipes. At one point the smoking of clay pipes became so popular that a pipe cleaners' trade was established. It was thought important even then to have a clean pipe, and periodically one's pipes were bundled together on a special stand and sent to the bakehouse for purification.

Clay-pipe smoking acquired its own

Portraits of Empress Eugénie of France (top l.), Earl Roberts of Kandahar, a hero of Indian and Boer wars, and Buffalo Bill adorn bowls of vintage 19th-century clays. Right: Garden-variety clays. Except for classic form at lower left, all are molded and glazed in stock designs.

traditions and lent itself to the realm of social custom and ritual. There was, for example, a special pipe for bridegrooms that was smoked the night of the wedding for good luck. It was not smoked again, but was put in a special case and hung on the wall. (One "wedding pipe" which survives is thirty-six inches long and decorated with copper leaves standing away from the stem.)

In the New World, too, smoking a pipe became an integral part of the thinking man's life. A story in Washington Irving's satirical *History of New York* deals with the extremes to which colonists would go to protect their freedom to smoke. During the reign of Willem Kieft ("William the Testy") as governor of New Netherland in the first half of the seventeenth century, a great fury was raised among the Dutch colonists when the governor issued an edict prohibiting the smoking of tobacco. As Irving tells it:

"Wilhelmus Kieft, as has already been observed, was a great legislator on a small scale, and had a microscopic eye in pub-

Preceding pages: Protesting Governor Willem Kieft's ban on smoking, burghers of New Netherland park on the gubernatorial doorstep puffing their beloved clays in George Boughton's "Edict of William the Testy Against Tobacco." Left: Gouda clays ready for kiln. Above: Trademarks of Gouda pipemakers' guild.

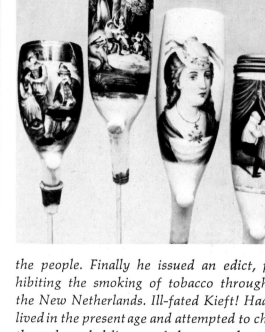

lic affairs. He had been greatly annoyed by the factious meeting of the good people of New Amsterdam, but, observing that on these occasions the pipe was ever in their mouth, he began to think that the pipe was at the bottom of the affair, and that there was some mysterious affinity between politics and tobacco smoke. Determined to strike at the root of the evil, he began forthwith to rail at tobacco, as a noxious, nauseous weed, filthy in all its uses; and as to smoking, he denounced it as a heavy tax upon the public pocket—a vast consumer of time, a great encourager of idleness, and a deadly bane to the prosperity and morals of

the people. Finally he issued an edict, prohibiting the smoking of tobacco throughout the New Netherlands. Ill-fated Kieft! Had he lived in the present age and attempted to check the unbounded license of the press, he could not have struck more sorely upon the sensibilities of the million. The pipe, in fact, was the great organ of reflection and deliberation of the New Netherlander. It was his constant companion and solace: was he gay, he smoked; was he sad, he smoked; his pipe was never out of his mouth; it was a part of his physiognomy; without it his best friends would not know him. Take away his pipe? You might as

Young man in Richard Woodville's painting, "The Cardplayers," holds a typical 19th-century porcelain pipe with china bowl, cherry-wood stem, and amber bit. Below: Staffordshire porcelain "puzzle" pipe, an example of 18th-century fancy. Above: Porcelain bowls with hand-painted designs.

well take away his nose!

"The immediate effect of the edict of William the Testy was a popular commotion. A vast multitude, armed with pipes and tobacco-boxes, and an immense supply of ammunition, sat themselves down before the governor's house, and fell to smoking with tremendous violence. The testy William issued forth like a wrathful spider, demanding the reason of this lawless fumigation. The sturdy rioters replied by lolling back in their seats, and puffing away with redoubled fury, raising such a murky cloud that the governor was fain to take refuge in the interior of his castle.

"A long negotiation ensued through the medium of Antony the Trumpeter. The governor was at first wrathful and unyielding, but was gradually smoked into terms. He concluded by permitting the smoking of tobacco, but he abolished the fair long pipes used in the days of Wouter Van Twiller, denoting ease, tranquillity, and sobriety of deportment; these he condemned as incompatible with the dispatch of business, in place whereof he substituted little captious short pipes, two inches in length, which, he observed, could be stuck in one corner of the mouth, or twisted in the hatband, and would never be in the way. Thus ended this alarming insurrection, which was long known by the name of The Pipe-Plot, and which, it has been somewhat quaintly observed, did end, like most plots and seditions, in mere smoke."

In the eighteenth century porcelain pipes took their place beside the standard clays. The bowls of the two were shaped very much the same, but the porcelains were larger and, rather than being of one piece as were the clays, porcelain bowls were made to fit vertical wood or wood-and-bone stems that reached three or four feet in length. (In early pipe design, length of stem alone served to cool the smoke.) Far more elaborately decorated than standard clays, porcelain bowls often had hand-painted scenes, portraits of monarchs, religious symbols, or mottoes in single or multiple colors. Many were fitted with wind caps of elaborate design. A small Kaiser helmet with a spike on top is the cap for one very long German pipe dating from just before World War I. Now in the private collection of Fred C. Diebel in Kansas City, Missouri, it is a cavalry-unit pipe depicting exploits in gold leaf and bright colors around the bowl and recording the names of the unit's officers at the back of the bowl above the shank.

There are a great many porcelain pipes available in the U. S. today, both in shapes similar to those typical of briars and also in the style of the old, long-stemmed, porcelain-bowled leisure pipes. The standard-shaped porcelain pipes come principally from the Royal Goedewaagen factory in Gouda, the Netherlands, and are offered in a variety of artistic finishes, ranging from pure white to a stain resembling the reddish-brown of a well-

Porcelains with decorated bowls and cherry-wood stems. Large bowl, which has capacity of at least two ounces, is in one piece, but those at left and right are articulated. Wind cap (center) was an 18th-century device to insure a "fireproof" smoke.

seasoned meerschaum. This factory also makes the famous Baronite pipe, which is a double-walled porcelain pipe. One of the major disadvantages of porcelain pipes, as with clays, is that they become extremely hot, making them difficult to hold. The air space between the inner and outer bowl walls of the notable Baronite acts an an insulator, keeping the bowl cooler and more comfortable in the hand. The air space also increases the dryness of the smoke, an effect also found in the calabash gourd pipe.

There are also copies of antique porcelain pipes to be had. The most beautiful and durable of these come from factories in Germany and Yugoslavia where special attention is given to creating exceptionally well-painted scenes and designs.

There are few good Dutch clay pipes available in the United States. Most are not glazed or coated at the tip and show little evidence that care has been taken in making them. However the excellent Goedewaagen pipes are now being imported again.

Clay pipes will endure abuse from hard smoking because of their resistance to burning out (they are comparable to the meerschaum in that respect). One must be very careful, however, not to allow great amounts of carbon to build up on the inner walls of clay or porcelain pipes because they will crack much faster than briars under similar conditions. And they do offer that special earthy

taste. The popularity of the clay pipe began to decline shortly after World War I. The life style was changing, and more practical, durable pipes were needed which could be carried easily and were more comfortable to hold. Briar, which had come on the scene in the 1850s, satisfied this demand. Clay pipes, along with the leisurely life they symbolized, became increasingly part of the past.

Softwood Pipes

There is little actual evidence to support the premise that smoking pipes were made from standard forest woods before the nineteenth century, but it seems logical because wood, plentiful in most parts of the world, has been a medium for artistic work, both primitive and refined, for thousands of years. It is probable that pipe bowls were carved from various woods by many peasants and primitive tribesmen, but because wood is so susceptible to the elements few examples remain.

Although stone and pottery pipes have survived, it is thought that the American Indians at the time of the explorers largely smoked wood pipes. One example we do have is the Walter Raleigh pipe in the Dunhill Collection in London, which was made in the New World from what appears to have been the forked branch of a small tree.

In the nineteenth century, woodcarvers in Europe started making elm, oak, and walnut pipe bowls similar in design to

Group of Royal Copenhagen porcelains made of blue and white delftware in standard briar shapes. All-white "golfer" (top l.) is presumably designed for convenient smoking on the links.

Above: Squire Jack Porter puffs a homey corncob in "Independence," a 19th-century painting by the American artist, Frank B. Mayer. Right: Old-time corncobs from Brussels Exposition of 1887 are handiwork of the Missouri Meerschaum Company, mass producers of "barnyard briars."

the porcelain bowls used in the long, wood-stemmed pipes. Also during this time men who, probably because of their poverty, had been fitting short wooden stems to the bowls of broken clay pipes began to produce small pipes from cherry and apple wood. In a similar way, corncob and hickory-wood pipes were developed in the central United States. What had been invented for home consumption out of necessity became widely popular. Necessity took on a different guise during World War II, when many briar-pipe manufacturers, unable to get briar from the Mediterranean areas, resorted to some of the softer woods. Pipes made from rosewood, cherry, and hickory are still in enough demand to justify production. They have remained somewhat popular probably because of their rather novel appearance and because they are relatively inexpensive.

The only type of softwood pipe I recommend is the cherry-wood. Some mature smokers may recall the massive cherry-wood pipes used by tobacconists as advertisements years ago. Made from sections of tree trunks, including bark, these models had large bowls bored in the tops and straight, hollow cherry branches fitted in the sides for stems. The cherry-wood pipes of today resemble those old pipes in many ways, though now they are always fitted at the tip of the stem with a vulcanite mouthpiece. There are some types today, known as one-piece pipes, which are made, as are briar pipes, with bowl and shank cut to-

Left: Cherry-wood pipes with bark left intact to help counter tendency of wood to split from cake buildup and heat of burning tobacco. Above: "James Wright" poses with simple corncob in Thomas Eakins painting.

63

gether and then fitted with vulcanite stems.

Softwood pipes, although they have a tendency to burn through rather rapidly under normal smoking conditions and although they never provide the smoker with the polished taste he experiences with a well-seasoned briar-root pipe, produce an interesting, woody-tasting smoke which is quite pleasing to those who smoke them regularly. The main producer of cherry-wood pipes imported by U. S. companies is the Ropp Pipe Company in France. Ropp's pipes are extremely well-crafted, yet inexpensive.

The Narghile and the Hookah

Water pipes—which include the narghile, hookah, and hubble-bubble—had their origin in Africa where they were used principally for smoking hemp. The narghile (the name is derived from the Indian word for "coconut") was the first of the water pipes.

In its original form, it is composed of a coconut shell partially filled with water, two tubes or reeds, a stem, and a clay bowl. One tube from the clay bowl runs through a long, two- to three-foot stem down into the coconut shell below the water line. A second reed or tube is fitted into the side of the shell above the water line. The smoker draws in smoke from this second tube, the smoke traveling from the bowl, where the tobacco burns, down the first tube, through the water where it is cooled and made softer, and then, ulti-

mately, reaching the smoker's mouth.

The popularity of this type of pipe grew rapidly and it spread throughout Africa, the Middle East, and the Far East, for use in smoking drugs as well as tobacco. The water pipe came to India during the earliest days of tobacco smoking there. Maharajahs saw these pipes as objects suitable for elaborate decoration and as a new symbol of luxury. By the eighteenth century, Indian ladies could hardly bear to part from their pipes, leaving them in their mouths as they bathed or were embraced by their lovers. The narghile outgrew the coconut base when it spread beyond the African villages of its origins, but the bulbous water-holding base of the pipe has always remained, even though other materials, such as terra cotta or clay, are used.

Several pipe designs have evolved from this basic water pipe. Chief among these is the hookah, which is generally elegant in design, with a fancy glass bottle or vase as a base. The Chinese have generally preferred to use some type of metal for the bowl and for the portion of the pipe which contains the water. Their pipes traditionally have been six to eight inches tall and portable. Countless smaller types (three to six inches high) have been created from brass throughout the years, particularly in the Middle East and India. In the last few years the Japanese have been creating small, unusual water pipes of glass or porcelain with wooden bowls and brass tubing.

Oriental Flavor: Intricately designed metal bowls—filagreed, painted, and enameled—elevate these Chinese bubble pipes into exquisite works of art. Tobacco (sometimes mixed with opium) goes in small upright tube.

In countries where the narghile and hookah are novelties, smoking them is an interesting experience. Water pipes are without question the coolest and driest-smoking pipes made, but as the smoke is drawn through the water it loses much of its characteristic taste. This is the reason many people prefer to mix a liqueur or spirits with the water in order to create an unusual flavor or to fortify a tobacco taste that otherwise would be rather bland.

A hookah or narghile, if well-designed and well-crafted, is a fine addition to the avid pipe smoker's collection, for decoration if for no other reason. Water pipes—manufactured in different sizes from a wide variety of materials—are available in many tobacco shops. One should take care to buy pipes that have good, sound fittings, for many modern water pipes are not sturdy. The finest pipes of traditional design are imported from West Germany. Because of their threaded horn connecting pieces and carefully designed hand-blown glass bottles, they are somewhat more expensive, but they are also more beautiful and reliable.

The Meerschaum Pipe

One of the most beautiful and interesting pipes a smoker can have in his collection is a well-crafted block meerschaum, whether of plain design or adorned with highly detailed carving. Since meerschaum's introduction as a material for pipes hundreds of years ago,

Sensual aura of Eugène Delacroix's "Women of Algiers" is heightened by presence of ubiquitous narghile, an indulgence of Muslim women of leisure, as well as of men. Originating probably in Africa, narghile cleanses and cools smoke as it passes through water.

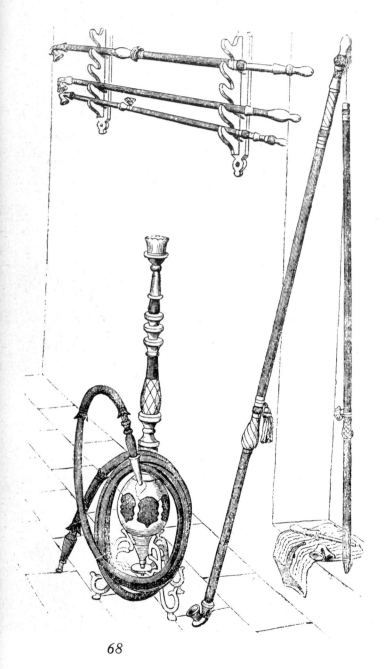

smokers have been intrigued and delighted by its unique quality of coloring. Delicate and seemingly translucent shades change into fascinating mottled pools of pink, amber, and red as the pipe is smoked. Meerschaum is no less alluring today than it was years ago, when Victorian gentlemen gathered in smoking rooms and compared their abilities to season their pipes.

A new meerschaum pipe is generally either pure white or a very pale, creamy yellow color. As it is smoked, tars and oils seep closer to the waxed surface of the shank and then the bowl. Pinks dissolve into deepening amber reds and the golds become a richer, golden brown. The coloring ultimately approaches black-brown or a muted, dark cherry. These changes take place very gradually, the seasoning progressing so slowly that it almost goes unnoticed. It is as if one were watching a very cautious but exquisite autumn slip stealthily into its colors. In addition to its beauty, the meerschaum smokes quite dryly and, after a time, tobacco smoked in it tastes somewhat more delicate and sweeter than it does in a briar.

Although there is some evidence that Turks were making pipe bowls from meerschaum in the mid-1600s, credit for introducing this mineral as a pipe material is generally given to Hungary. In the early eighteenth century, Count Andrassy, a noble from Budapest who was an envoy to Turkey, brought home

Narghile and Chibouks: Turkish delights depicted in 19th-century engraving (l.). Right: Ottoman in Delacroix's "Turque Fumant Assis sur un Divan" enjoys a pipeful of toombak, *an aromatic mixture likely to include aloe, rose leaves, and opium or hashish, along with tobacco.*

69

with him a present of two blocks of meer-schaum. He gave them to a cobbler, Karl Kowates, who, as the story goes, was also a skilled wood-carver, and commissioned him to make a pair of tobacco pipes from the blocks. In time the cobbler presented the pipes to Andrassy who, in turn, gave one back in payment for his labors. Several weeks went by during which time Kowates smoked his new pipe while working on boots. One day he ac-cidentally rubbed some of his cobbler's bees-wax on a portion of the pipe. After a time he noticed that the wax had improved the meer-schaum's ability to color and he covered the entire pipe with it. Later he noticed that the beeswax also had improved the flavor of the smoke. These first European meerschaums soon proved their excellence. Andrassy was as delighted as Kowates, more meerschaum was imported from Turkey, and before long many of Andrassy's friends also were enjoying meerschaums made by the cobbler. This, at any rate, is the accepted tale.

No matter who actually was respon-sible for the introduction of the meerschaum pipe, it steadily gained favor among wealthy smokers throughout Europe. After 1750 pipes of the new material were in exceptionally heavy demand. Unlike clay, however, which was available to everyone, meerschaum was re-stricted to the rich and titled who could afford to commission the handiwork of a carver or an artist. In a romantic tale written in 1785 by the German author Heinrich Stilling, a char-acter searching for a token of friendship and great esteem believes that only meerschaum is a worthy gift. The meerschaum rapidly be-came the pipe of the stylish smoker and the effort and money spent by these smokers to outdo their peers probably accounts for the artistic meerschaums created in those times.

In many cases, the fact that these masterpieces are pipes is almost incidental; indeed, a great many never were smoked. Some of the very large, magnificent pieces adorned cabinets and shelves as objects of art. One wealthy Englishman had a lovely pipe made for himself even though he didn't smoke. When the pipemaker had finished the job, the gentleman instructed him to color the bowl before delivering it. For a period of two or three weeks, the pipe was smoked by every pipemaker in the shop until the color became very rich and dark. The gentleman was well pleased and promptly placed his seasoned treasure on the mantle.

As artisans and wood-carvers turned to pipemaking, they soon became swamped with more orders than they could fill. By the 1850s, enterprising merchants and pipemakers set up factories that employed hundreds of carvers. Between that time and the years just before World War I, when briar began to dominate the industry, the thousands of meer-schaum pipes created in factories finally found their way into the hands of middle-class

Fashionable lady in Jean Étienne Liotard's
"Turkish Lady with Her Attendant" pauses for a pipeful.
Her chibouk has three-part stem made of wood or
cane with overall length of four or
five feet, and ornamental clay bowl. Long
stem made tobacco smoke cooler.

72

Constantin Hansen's painting, "Reunion
of the Danish Artists in Rome,"
has dapper Danes sporting extremely long
Turkish chibouks and cigars at
gathering for afternoon smoke. Man at
left is satisfied with a small porcelain.

smokers, who now were able to indulge in what only nobles and the rich had been able to afford in previous years. Meerschaum pipes were produced in England, France, Germany, and Hungary, but the majority was carved in Vienna. That city was not only a manufacturing center but was long linked with the substance which provided the perfect mouthpiece for a meerschaum—amber.

During the meerschaum's almost two-hundred-year reign as the only luxury pipe, artisans produced two basic styles. The first was what we might call the "complete" pipe: An amber or amber-and-horn stem was fitted to the shank of the pipe and secured with a threaded bone connector. This stem flowed with the lines of the pipe. The second, although beautiful and elaborate, was nothing more than a bowl with a rather short, sturdy shank with a smooth, tapered hole bored at the butt into which could be fitted a cork or leather-tipped wooden stem. The stems, which were manufactured in various lengths, were generally made of cherry wood and had a macaroni-shaped mouthpiece.

Today, with the exception of the fine carved heads produced by Andreas Bauer in Vienna, almost all meerschaum pipes are fashioned into shapes corresponding to those of standard briar pipes. In marked contrast, those carved by artisans years ago featured clusters of exquisite figures in relief or forming the entire body of the pipe. The bowl often was slipped in unobtrusively so as to avoid disrupting a battle scene, or dancing nymphs pouring wine for an amber-faced Bacchus.

Though there generally is a lack of intricate carving on pipes produced today, this is by no means an indication of inferiority. Styles have changed. Plain pipes are more popular among twentieth-century smokers who find the styles of the past ostentatious. It is also a question of supply. Intricately designed pipes are rare today because it is difficult to get exceptionally large meerschaum blocks such as those that were available a hundred years ago. Highly skilled men and women in Europe and the United States still produce fine block-meerschaum pipes, and meerschaums, no matter what their size and shape, continue to color and season beautifully.

Meerschaum is a German word meaning "sea foam"— it derived its name because it often was seen floating on the Black Sea. The German term probably has been used because German-speaking people controlled the meerschaum-pipe industry until World War II. Also, most of the craftsmen who began making meerschaum pipes in the United States came from either Germany or Austria.

Meerschaum is a very soft, porous, hydrous silicate of magnesia that is found in pockets within clay or serpentine deposits. Its origin is unknown, but it is believed to have been formed from the metamorphic shells and bones of tiny prehistoric sea creatures. Its geological name, assigned in the mid-nineteenth century by a German mineralogist, is sepiolite, from the Greek "Sepio," or cuttlefish bone, which it resembles.

While deposits are found in many areas of the world, including England, Greece, Spain, Morocco, and Arizona and South Carolina, the quality meerschaum used by the pipe industry comes mainly from Turkey and, to a lesser degree, from Tanzania. Meerschaum from other areas is either of such poor quality or available in such small quantities that it is not profitable to mine it. The very finest grades come from Turkey and are mined on the plains of Eskisehir, west of Ankara.

Large chunks are dug from pits, or galleries, one hundred and fifty to three hundred and fifty feet below the surface. The chunks are a dingy, mottled gray and white, covered with clay or with bits of serpentine imbedded in them as the result of intense pressure. For pipemaking, the best blocks generally come from deep within these chunks where the meerschaum is relatively free of impurities, such as sand, and structurally weak areas which crumble when carved.

These crude chunks must have their useless outer portion removed. The mineral is moist and malleable when it is taken from the ground, which facilitates cutting. After the chunks have been cleaned, they are sanded into rough white blocks and allowed to dry in the sun or in a warm room for two to three

Clay pipe in hand, woodchopper-boatman of George C. Bingham's "The Wood Boat" (1850) rests on shore. Crew of flatboat will soon depart to sell his stacked cordwood, already on board, at communities along rivers of middle America.

weeks until all moisture has evaporated. Then they are inspected, and impurities or flaws are removed. Occasionally, large blocks must be cut into several smaller ones because of interior weaknesses.

When the blocks are dry and free of obvious flaws, they are waxed and polished. This step enables the expert grader to judge more clearly the texture of the mineral. Grading takes into account porosity, color, weight, and consistency of texture. There are five final grades, the highest being pure white, very light in weight, and extremely porous. After the quality of each piece is determined, the grades are divided according to block size. Then they are packed into heavy wooden cases for shipment.

At the factories, the blocks are examined and organized by sizes and grades corresponding to the pipes which are to be made. Just prior to use, the blocks are soaked in water for thirty minutes to an hour, depending on size, to soften them and facilitate the cutting; meerschaum creates less dust as it is being worked when moist than when dry. Timing is crucial here. A piece of meerschaum can absorb more than its weight in water, but if left to soak too long it will break up into useless little pieces.

The first man to handle the blocks is a "rough-in" man. His job is to cut down the blocks with a band saw and a special knife until they roughly resemble the desired shapes. Next, an experienced man trims the bowl more precisely until it is very near the final shape. The master pipemaker of the factory takes the roughly finished bowls and turns them on a wooden, foot-operated lathe until they are perfectly shaped and free of rough edges. Mastery of this difficult operation takes many years' practice. Great skill is required to operate the foot pedal on the pipemaker's lathe and at the same time coordinate the pressure and angle of the various chisels. One slip of the cutting knife can destroy the entire bowl. This series of operations is extremely exacting, yet experienced pipemakers can work with amazing rapidity while maintaining a high level of quality.

From the first cutting until the master pipemaker finishes the work on the lathe, great care is taken to save every scrap of meerschaum. This is ultimately sold to manufacturers who use it for pressed meerschaum pipes.

After the basic shape has been formed, the bowl of the pipe is bored and the channel from the shank to the inside of the bowl is drilled. Then the bowls are placed in a drying room or a low-temperature oven for six to twelve hours, depending on how moist they are. Drying the pipes after cutting is extremely important for it hardens the meerschaum. Hardened meerschaum more readily holds a high luster, and the pores when free of moisture readily absorb the beeswax coating.

Bowls are next fitted with threaded bone connectors. Then Bakelite or, less frequently today, amber stems are hand-cut to fit the shanks and are screwed down over the connectors. The nearly finished pipes are set aside at this point until the cement holding the connectors into the shanks hardens. The pipes are sanded with sharkskin to remove any striations or small scratches on the bowls. Finally, they are polished with a dried grass, such as bulrush. Meerschaum is so soft that the use of any other polishing agent, such as pumice, tripoli, or jewelers' rouges, would score the pipe and make it worthless.

Now the pipes are boiled in white beeswax for three to five minutes, after which they are placed on wire racks that hold them by the inner bowls so they dry evenly. When dry, the pipes are polished with a soft cloth and packed for shipment. Wax not only contributes to the product's appearance, giving the pipes a fine luster, but it is needed to seal the bowls, to hold in the tars and oils which color the pipes and which also affect the taste of tobaccos smoked in them. As these tars and oils build up inside the wall and shank of the pipe, the smoker will notice that the smoke becomes sweeter and more flavorful.

There are three basic kinds of meerschaum pipes available today: pressed meerschaum, hardened, precolored African block meerschaum, and pure white meerschaum from Turkish blocks. Each type has advantages and disadvantages one must consider before buying.

Pressed meerschaum is the least ex-

"Columbus Coming to the New World,"
a masterpiece of meerschaum carving made
for the 1893 Columbian Exposition at Chicago.
Bowl is an insert in the shape of a palm tree.
(Note fronds at left.) Stem is made of
alternating bands of light and dark amber.

*Details of "Columbus" pipe on preceding
page. Columbus (l.) claims continent
for Ferdinand and Isabella of Spain.
Top: Members of expedition gaze in awe at
New World, while zealous missionary
(bottom) converts heathen Indians.*

pensive. Rather than being carved or turned from a solid, natural block, pressed meerschaums are manufactured from "pseudoblocks"—finely ground meerschaum scraps mixed with a binding substance, pressed into blocks which are allowed to harden. Almost all of these pipes are precolored and have a rather solid texture that looks more like polished, stained plaster of Paris than meerschaum. Unlike natural block meerschaum, which is exceptionally porous and light in weight, pressed types usually are dense and rather heavy. The density of pressed meerschaum prevents pipes made of it from coloring in an attractive way, the reason most of these pipes are stained. There is little basis for comparison between such a pipe and a fine block meerschaum, which takes a great deal of smoking time to color but which rewards all effort.

Nevertheless, if one still is interested in trying a pressed meerschaum pipe, he will find the type identified in the following ways: pressed meerschaum, Vienna meerschaum, "real" meerschaum, and "genuine" meerschaum. Fine, natural, unpressed meerschaums *always* are classified as "block meerschaum." The only pressed meerschaum I recommend is that used in the Andreas Bauer and Pioneer calabash pipes. Pioneer's bowl, while it is little softer than most other compressed types, is remarkably light and, surprisingly enough, colors rather well.

During the past few years, increasing numbers of pipes made of meerschaum mined in Africa—principally in Tanzania—have been imported into the U.S. While most of these pipes are made in Africa, some of the medium-priced varieties are produced by manufacturers in other countries.

African meerschaum pipes seldom cost more than $25, yet they smoke similarly to fine Turkish block meerschaums. They are extremely durable. Thanks to the free-turning metal connector, or military mounting, which is used in these pipes, it is impossible for the stems to be worn out of alignment. They smoke dryly. And because of the hardening agent with which they are glazed, the bowls may be held in the hand without fear of soiling or discoloring the finish. They can be found in three different finishes, all of which are precolored or stained. The smooth, natural finish in some ways resembles a virgin block meerschaum that is about half-colored; the other two finishes are rough reliefs—one is black, the other yellowish. One of the major disadvantages of these lightly precolored African meerschaum pipes is that they will not absorb color from tobacco tars as delicately as the virgin pipes made from the more porous Turkish meerschaum. They also tend to be somewhat heavier.

These pipes are excellent for smokers who prefer the dryness of meerschaum but cannot afford the fine virgin pipes. Also Afri-

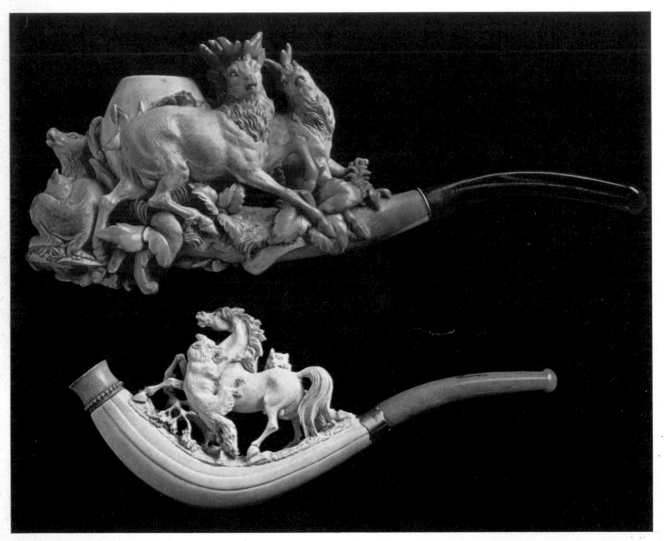

*Typical of 19th-century meerschaum art
are wildlife scenes on smoked pipe (top) and
unsmoked cigar holder (bottom).
Right: Meerschaum bowls, c. 1900.
Note smoked head of West Indian (top center) and
bull's horns and stem made of amber.*

can meerschaums make excellent stand-ins for times when one would like to smoke a meerschaum, but is afraid that it might be damaged.

While they are not so elaborate as the old meerschaums, today's virgin block-meerschaum pipes with smaller carved motifs and in briar shapes are no less beautiful or well-crafted than their fine meerschaum ancestors were at the height of their glory in the 1850s. Unlike the sturdier pressed and African meerschaums, fine virgin meerschaum pipes are delicate and demand respect. If proper care is taken, they will smoke excellently and beautify a pipe collection for many years.

These block meerschaums are left pure in color—they are never stained—and are available in three different finishes. The carved pipes can be found adorned with any number of motifs, from heads of long-bearded sheiks, old seamen, queens, even Mephistopheles, to classics such as a hawk's talons grasping an egg or a hand holding a skull (probably inspired by *Hamlet*).

The second variety is the smooth finish, which colors beautifully. The third is the relief, or rough, meerschaum, which is tooled, sandblasted, or made into a network of canals with a dental burr. Because of its

Classic myth of Leda and the Swan is perpetuated in meerschaum on cigar holder at far left; buxom nude serves as figurehead for pipe at right. Above: Handsome but more mundane pipe has hunters returning with deer.

appearance, this is called the "coral finish." These generally are made from smooth-finished pipes in which some small fissures and sandpits were discovered. In creating the coral finish such superficial imperfections are removed and the pipe is rendered flawless. Relief-finished block meerschaums color in a beautiful and unusual way. The surfaces of the relief cause more contrast in color as the pipe is smoked. First very delicate rose shades appear deep in the carving contrasting with the creamy outer surface. Then as the pipe is seasoned, mellow amber shades appear, first deep in the carving, then on the surface. Generally these relief-finished block meerschaums are lighter in weight than the smooth varieties.

These pipes usually are fitted with Bakelite or amber stems which are connected by means of a bone screw. The one exception is a pipe made by the Andreas Bauer Company in Vienna in which a Teflon tenon in the stem fits into a collar of the same material in the end of the shank. This kind of connector eliminates the possibility of overturning the stem and forcing it out of alignment. It also guards against broken connectors or shanks.

When selecting a meerschaum, make sure there are no striations on the bowl, shank, or stem. Small scratches can show up dramatically when the pipe begins to color. Look for a pipe that is light in weight for its size; it will be more comfortable and, in most cases, more porous and thus will smoke drier and

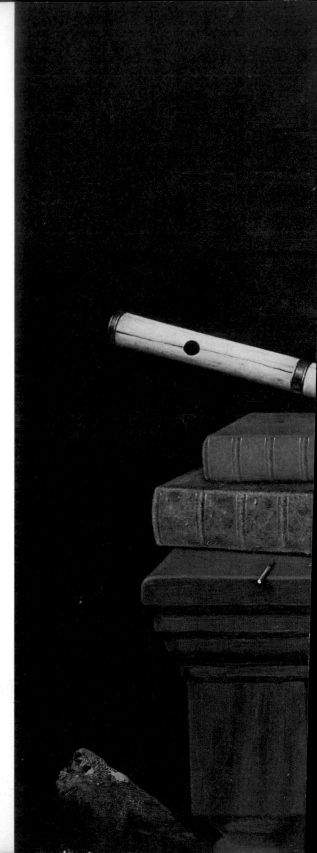

Glowing embers of well-seasoned meerschaum with cherry-wood stem and amber bit scorch a copy of the New York Sun *in William Harnett's trompe-l'oeil painting, "Emblems of Peace." Stringy tobacco in blue box appears to be a fine-cut Virginia.*

color more beautifully. If the pipe has a bone connector make sure it fits tightly and is properly aligned when it is flush with the shank—not turned to one side or the other. Pipes with amber bits are rather hard to find, but usually can be ordered if they are not stocked. One might hesitate to opt for the amber, though. They are more expensive and more fragile than Bakelite stems.

Materials for the finest meerschaums come from Turkey; finished virgin-type pipes do also, but in most cases they are inferior to those made in Europe and the United States. The craftsmanship by and large is sloppy. Scratches are often left on the bowl and shank, the draft hole in many cases is bored off-center, and the bit work is seldom symmetrical and well-polished. They are not as expensive as fine Viennese and American block-meerschaum pipes, but when you find a nice one it smokes and colors very well. Most smokers have no more than two meerschaums in their collection, and the man who is making his first purchase would do well to choose a well-crafted pipe, one that will perform excellently. It may cost a bit more, but it will be well worth the money spent.

Caring for a meerschaum pipe is easy if the smoker realizes that it is very delicate. It can be cleaned and smoked like any other pipe, but very little char should be allowed to build up because the meerschaum bowl will split under the pressure of a thick

Hunter and his dog, alert for game,
are carved on shank of elegant pipe at left.
Sea nymphs above romp on a stylized
shell. Both illustrate the fanciful work
done on meerschaums in the mid-19th century,
heyday of master carvers.

cake. When using a pipe cleaner to swab out the shank and stem, one should be extremely careful not to run the stiff wire end of the cleaner into the soft meerschaum at the bottom of the bowl as this can eventually wear a small hole through the bottom of the pipe. When emptying ashes from a block-meerschaum pipe, one should never pound them out. It is much better to turn the bowl upside down over an ashtray and scoop out the remaining tobacco ashes with a pipe tool. Overturning the pipe this way also will keep any juices that are left in the bottom of the bowl from touching the outside of the pipe and discoloring the finish.

One should always hold the pipe by the stem, if possible, or if this is difficult, the smoker should cut a piece of chamois and sew it around the bowl, leaving it there until the pipe has colored. The wax finish is extremely delicate. It soils and scratches easily.

The stem of a pipe with a bone connector, should be removed as infrequently as possible to prevent wear. A worn connector might ultimately loosen the stem or cause it to overturn. When the smoker does take the stem off, he should do so only when the pipe is completely dry. When putting it back on the pipe, hold the shank straight up and turn the stem slowly down until it begins to tighten, then gently move it into proper alignment. Replacing the stem in this manner will prevent overturning and breaking the connector or shank.

"Nelson Pipe" has fallen admiral (far l.)
wounded in Hardy's arms in Battle at the Nile.
Allegorical figure of Britannia as a sea goddess
decorates the wind cap. Top: Amber pipe
in the shape of a bull's head. Bottom:
Meerschaum bowl encrusted with gems.

91

Turn-of-the-century ad for "Happy Dream" pipe tobacco promised the smoker fantastic visions of pleasure from a Virginia cut plug. Right: Smoked meerschaum in another trompe-l'oeil painting by William Harnett (1893).

If for some reason the pipe should be thrown out of alignment, or the connector should break, or a stem that has been bitten through must be replaced, take the pipe to a reputable tobacco shop before trying any Rube Goldberg techniques of your own. Do-it-yourself repairing has broken and disfigured many beautiful pipes so badly that they couldn't be saved, even by an excellent pipe-maker.

To color a meerschaum pipe one needn't rely on any sixteenth-century alchemist's techniques. Just smoke the pipe and be patient. Naturally, the more one smokes his pipe the more tars and oils will be absorbed and the faster the pipe will color. It generally takes two or three years for a pipe to darken to a rich brown or cherry amber. One should keep in mind that pipes with thin walls and shanks color faster than sturdier, thicker ones. I suggest that a smoker cover the bowl of his pipe with a chamois glove. This will protect the bowl without affecting its ability to color.

If one's patience does run out, there is a trick for speeding the coloring process which will not harm the pipe in any way—though it might raise a few eyebrows among stone-faced connoisseurs. Take a long hose from a hookah and tape it to the bit end of the pipe so that smoke can be drawn through it freely. Next, fill the pipe with tobacco and light and tamp it as usual, making certain no tobacco can expand and fall out onto the bowl

when it is relighted. Now, take a clean kitchen towel that has been folded to a narrow width. Wrap this tightly around the stem of the pipe, making sure the towel covers no portion of the meerschaum. Then stuff the pipe, bowl first, into a large glass tumbler using the bulky towel to stop up the end of the glass and also to hold the pipe in the center of the container. Place some heavy object on either side of the glass to keep it from rolling and begin smoking the pipe vigorously, occasionally blowing gently back through the bowl to keep the interior of the glass thick with hot smoke. Be very careful not to blow back so hard that ashes fall out over the bowl, which will be rather sticky with warm wax.

After smoking for a while, you will notice condensation forming on the inside of the glass. Make sure the pipe does not touch this moisture. If it appears that some of the moisture may drop onto the bowl, pull the towel and pipe out, wipe out the glass, and begin again. After five or six bowls smoked in this manner, the smoker will notice his pipe coloring very rapidly, as tars and oils are being absorbed from both the inside and outside of the pipe.

This process makes the pipe extremely hot and most of the original wax finish will evaporate. When the smoker has completed this "bottle smoking," he should take some white beeswax and, using an alcohol flame which contains no soot, allow droplets of the wax to fall all over the pipe. Pass the bowl and shank of the pipe over this alcohol flame just long enough to allow the wax to melt and spread over their surfaces. When the pipe and wax have cooled, the bowl should be rubbed with a clean, soft cloth until the original luster reappears. This whole operation, though it works, is rather tricky and, frankly, I would hesitate before subjecting my only $65 Andreas Bauer to it.

The following are some fine meerschaum pipe manufacturers: Manxland, Pioneer, Barling, and Amboseli for African meerschaums; Andreas Bauer, Paul Fischer, and Pioneer for virgin block meerschaums.

The Calabash Pipe

The calabash is a beautiful and highly functional pipe. It is light in weight, making it exceptionally comfortable to hold in the hand or mouth. Because of the pipe's bent design and the large air space within the hollow, absorbent gourd separating the bowl from the stem, the smoke is very cool and dry. The calabash is never hot to the touch. Furthermore, its shape and color are pleasing to the eye—its colors slowly deepen in shades of amber, first mottled and light, then darkening to red amber, until finally it reaches a mellow, almost translucent reddish brown-black.

No one knows who was responsible for the first calabash gourds reaching European pipemakers' hands, but it would be reasonable to assume the Dutch had something to do with it. Conceivably, anyone visiting Cape Town, South Africa, in the mid-seventeenth century could have observed natives smoking gourd pipes and brought the idea back home, but let's let the Dutch have the credit. The natives' pipes were not unlike our modern calabashes, although they were not as refined. The native calabash dacca, or hemp, pipe is made from a club- or bottle-shaped gourd, which has been scooped out and dried. A bowl, clay in most cases, is connected to the top of the bulbous portion of the gourd by means of a tube. The pipe then is fitted at the neck with a long wooden or gourd stem. The pipe is generally two to three feet in length.

Almost two hundred and fifty years elapsed between the Dutch discovery of the African calabash pipe and the early 1900s when the pipe was finally refined and became popular in England, Europe, and the United States. The gourd itself was a useful utensil on both sides of the Atlantic from the sixteenth century at least. In a 1597 herbal we read of common use of the rind as a receptacle for oils, honey, and other fluids; in his *Travels in North America*, Peter Kalm in 1750 reported seeing such "shells" scraped clean and used as ladles and bowls. John Gerard's *Herball*, published in 1636, probably contains the first description of the preparation of calabash as pipemakers know it: "The Gourd groweth into any fashion that you would have

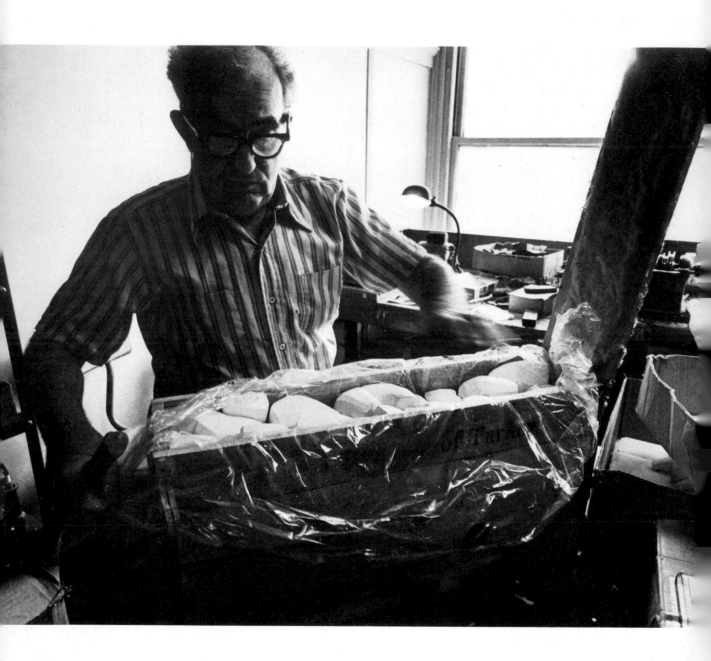

it...according to the mold wherein it is put while it is yong."

The particular gourd used by the pipemaking industry is a single species of *Lagenaria*. Although this plant can be grown in many parts of the world virtually all of the gourds used by pipemakers come from Africa, where the growing conditions are ideal. It takes a great amount of heat and sunlight to mature these hard-shelled fruits.

The seedlings appear soon after planting and they closely resemble those of the cucumber. As the vines begin to spread, the plant develops large oval or kidney-shaped leaves six to ten inches in width. The fruit begin developing from white blossoms about two months after planting and before they begin to harden, while still tender, it is necessary to bend or shape the necks so the gourds will conform to the basic shape desired by the pipe manufacturers.

This shaping process is quite simple. The growing gourd is placed on a board that has been drilled with holes. Long pegs are placed in the board to form a pattern for bending the neck of the gourd. The gourd is bent slightly around the pattern pegs, and more pegs are placed in the board close to the outside of the neck in order to restrain it from returning to its normal position. After a day (or sometimes less), when the gourd has adjusted to the pressure of bending, the pegs are shifted and it is bent a little farther, and so on

Austrian pipemaker Paul Fischer (l.) examines a shipment of Turkish block meerschaum in his New York workshop. Using a band saw (top) and a coping saw (bottom), he cuts a block into pipe-size segments.

97

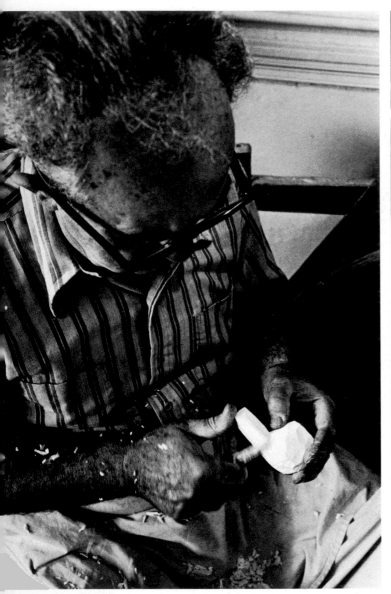

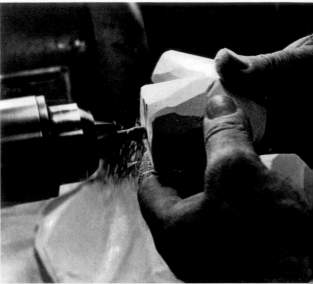

This page: Rough-shaping the bowl (l.) and drilling a centering hole (top) preparatory to detailed work on lathe. Above: Pipes with drilled bowls, ready to be turned. Right: Tools flanking Paul Fischer are used in such steps as shaping bowl (top l.) and boring air hole (top r.).

until the desired shape is attained. Generally, three or four gradual bendings are required. After the shaping is completed, the gourd is allowed to ripen in the sun, untouched except for an occasional turning to ensure an even color. When the gourds are ripe, they are harvested, and some of the roughness is lightly polished off. A man operating a saw cuts the necks of the gourds and scoops out the soft inner flesh and seeds, leaving the necks hollow, before they are again placed in the sun to dry thoroughly.

When the dried, seasoned gourd necks reach the factory, they are sorted according to size. The first step in manufacturing is the trueing up, or leveling off, of both ends of the neck by sanding. Then the hole at the small end of the neck is enlarged by drilling to accommodate the briar or vulcanite shank cap into which the stem will fit. Next, the large end of the gourd is reamed out in order to be fitted with a cork gasket which will hold the bowl more securely. The gourd is fitted with a shank cap which generally is oversized and must be turned or sanded to fit flush with the tip of the gourd. Then the pipe is fitted with a stem, and a cup (also called a "top bowl") of pressed or, occasionally, block meerschaum is fitted to the pipe. When a porcelain bowl is used, the cork gasket must be reamed out until the bowl fits properly. Polishing is all that remains before the finished pipe is boxed for shipment.

In selecting a calabash, one should look for a gourd that is straight—not tilted to one side, that is—and has a rather thick neck, for greater strength and durability. Such a neck does not constrict the smoke as much as a slender one and, because it generally has a thicker inner rind, will be more absorbent for a longer period of time and thus stand up well under heavy smoking. Size is not terribly important in calabashes unless one prefers a very short smoke or plans to carry the pipe with him. The smaller varieties have a reduced capacity for tobacco, but they are more comfortable to carry in the mouth and are less bulky in the pocket.

A calabash is a good smoking pipe from the beginning. It requires no "breaking in." From the first bowl the smoker can fill it to the top and smoke as though he has been enjoying the pipe for years, bowl after bowl throughout the day. After a time, however, if one smokes his calabash often, it will fill up with tar and moisture, as will any other pipe, and require a long rest. The calabash pipe is excellent for the new smoker who cannot afford to buy enough pipes for adequate rotation. If he has a calabash, he can smoke it for long periods of time between briars, which will give the briars more time to rest and dry out.

The calabash pipe, especially when it is new and absorbent, has a tendency to thin the taste of a tobacco. As the cells of the gourd fill with tars and become less absorbent, more flavor reaches the smoker. Though the cala-

Hand-turning a bowl. On stove at Fischer's right, water is being heated for bending stems, and beeswax melted for application of final satin coating. Completed pipes of assorted shapes are in box in foreground.

bash will never smoke quite as sweetly as a fine briar-root pipe, it has a taste of its own that is every bit as good. Some sensitive pipe smokers have been spoiled by these pipes. Rich or strong tobaccos they enjoyed but couldn't smoke regularly were toned down by the calabash just enough to make smoking them a pleasure.

Some of the first calabash pipes were rather crude. Although the best grades always have been fitted with block or compressed meerschaum smoking cups, in the early days there were a great number on the market with cups or bowls made of plaster of Paris, tin, and even briar. Fortunately, the major companies only use meerschaum cups. The two leading firms for fine calabash pipes today are the Pioneer Meerschaum Company in New York and Andreas Bauer in Vienna. Both produce calabash pipes with pressed meerschaum bowls. Pioneer also makes an inexpensive model with a porcelain bowl; however, I recommend only the meerschaum-bowl varieties. The Pioneer pipe is fitted with a fancy military bit that can be removed easily whether it is hot or cold. The Bauer pipe has the standard briar shank cap and is fitted with a plain vulcanite bit.

As far as cleaning and care are concerned, the calabash is similar to other pipes. It needs periods of rest and it should not be oversmoked. It is different from other pipes in that the calabash bowl should not be allowed to

cake up except for a bare covering. One cannot burn out a meerschaum smoking cup but it will crack faster than briar under pressure from carbon.

The inside of the gourd should be cleaned periodically. To do this, remove the stem and smoking cup, then pour some spirits or nonsweet pipe freshener into the large end of the gourd. Move the gourd about gently, as you would a brandy snifter, for a short while and then let it stand for a few minutes. During this time, the liquid will break down the tar deposits. After three or four minutes, pour the liquid out through the shank end to avoid getting it on the cork. Wipe off the shank cap and then stuff a soft cloth into the gourd to absorb any excess moisture. Remove the cloth and let the gourd dry overnight, or longer if necessary. If one smokes a calabash hard and often, this cleaning should be done regularly—about once a week.

After the pipe has been smoked regularly for a while, the smoker may notice the draft hole at the bottom of a meerschaum smoking cup becoming soft and dark. When this happens, take the smoking cup and turn it upside down, then subject the soft portion to the flame of your lighter until it supports a flame by itself. When the flame dies, let the bowl cool completely. This operation burns off the tar and hardens the tip, restoring it to its normal condition. If the tip of the bowl is allowed to remain soft, the meerschaum will

Modern calabash is characterized by inner bowl, or cup, of pressed meerschaum, standard briar shank to which neck of gourd is secured, and vulcanite stem designed to follow the natural curve of the gourd.

wear away when the smoker runs cleaners through the draft hole.

If a smoking cup is broken, remove all of the pieces from the pipe and take the gourd, not the broken bowl, to a tobacconist for shipment to the factory for replacement of the bowl. This will be done for a modest price.

If the gourd should be broken in two, there is a fairly dependable method of repairing it. Remove the stem and smoking cup from the pipe. Take three or four soft pipe cleaners and run them through both sections of the broken gourd, bending them over the shank cap. Now mix a small amount of epoxy glue in the normal way and cover both of the broken surfaces, making sure the glue does not get on the cleaners. At this point, join the two pieces of the pipe and bend the cleaners protruding from the large end of the gourd over it in order to pull the broken pieces tightly together and hold them in place. After doing this, place the gourd in a cradle (a small box filled with tissue or a lump of clay to stabilize the pipe will do the job). The cradle will allow the gourd to rest without strain on the broken area after it has been glued. After three or four days, remove the cleaners and peel away the excess glue. The pipe should be ready for use. This gluing method will not hold every break, but it has been successful in many cases. I have three calabashes that I have repaired in this way and they are as strong as they were the day they were purchased.

The Briar-Root Pipe

Once upon a time, a French envoy was traveling back to France from Geneva through the Jura Mountains when a fearful storm forced his party to seek refuge at an inn in the little town of St. Claude, in southeastern France. After eating the evening meal, he went to his room to get his meerschaum pipe and tobacco from his bag and found that the pipe had been broken during the rugged trip along the mountain roads.

Aware that the townspeople of St. Claude were skilled at carving and turning woods, he took the pipe to the innkeeper and asked if he knew someone who might be able to repair it. The old man said perhaps he could find someone. With the pieces of broken pipe in his coat pocket, he went to a friend who was one of the most skillful craftsmen in the village. The wood-carver looked at the shattered pipe and could think of no good way to repair it; yet, rather than displease the nobleman, he decided to make a pipe from wood. Realizing that the oak and walnut he had would never compare with the meerschaum, he took from the hearth where it had been seasoning a most unusual piece—a burl from the white heath, in French *bruyère*, which had been brought to him from the Mediterranean coast of France by his son. It looked like a large, rough, shelled nut. It was extremely hard and, because of its unusual looks, he thought it would make a novel pipe. The innkeeper was sent back to tell

"Since nature forms the gourd from which these pipes are made," an eminent craftsman points out, "no two calabashes are alike." Note sharp curve of the pipe in foreground. (Stem of pipe at left was twisted for convenience in taking picture.) Golden hue is sign of smoking age.

the nobleman that he would have to wait until morning for his pipe.

The count arose early for travel and found a tired wood-carver waiting for him downstairs. Apologizing for being unable to repair the meerschaum, he produced from a cloth bag the handsome pipe which had been made from the burl. The nut-shaped block had been brushed and polished with the gnarled crust left intact, a bowl had been bored in the top, and the amber stem from the meerschaum was fitted to it. The count was thrilled with this unusual pipe and immediately filled the bowl. As he smoked, his smiles of delight showed the company in the room that he was pleased with the service that had been rendered him. Before leaving St. Claude, the traveler paid the carver well and thanked him profusely for his efforts.

As time passed, more and more travelers began to inquire in St. Claude about the new wooden pipes made of the *bruyère*

Portraits in Briar: 19th-century character studies (above & top r.) include a bespectacled barrister, conquistador, and periwigged courtier. Bottom r.: "True Comfort" tobacco has benign effect on three cronies.

Artful briars above include three handsomely carved bowls, a smooth, short-stemmed, half-bent billiard, and (l.) an articulated porcelain-style pipe with cherry-wood stem. Right: Handcrafted briars. Note light color of the burl. Figurine match holders and tobacco tin are antiques.

root, and the carvers soon were engaged in a growing trade—one that would someday make the name of St. Claude synonymous with fine briar pipes.

This tale may be apocryphal, but the important point is that briar was introduced as material for pipes and eventually became the major pipe material. It is still generally regarded as the most successful. Briar's reputation grew slowly. Not until the 1850s were briar pipes produced on a large scale. As far as we can determine, a man named Comoy from St. Claude was the first to produce briars in quantity. Comoy took his pipemaking business to England, where meerschaums and cigars were the two most popular smokes of the day. People not only wanted to enjoy a quiet evening smoke in the drawing room, but they wanted to smoke on the move. Cigars were all right for this, but the intricately designed meerschaums were both cumbersome and easily broken.

Sweet-smoking, durable briar pipes had the capability of filling the need but they were not readily accepted. At first, they were similar in design to meerschaums, with gold caps and intricate carvings, but generally were considered to be poorer in quality. Meerschaums continued to lead the market.

The invention of power equipment for mass production of pipes in the early 1900s gave briars the boost they needed. The new machinery enabled pipemakers to design more

"Portrait of Soler," painted by Picasso in 1903, poses the subject, a Barcelona tailor, with a long-stemmed briar of the sort popular in 1850s. Right: Churchwarden briars, characterized by long, graceful stems and small bowls, were favored by fashionable smokers.

functional pipe shapes from briar. Soon the smaller, lighter, more durable briar pipes overtook meerschaums. Indeed, manufacturers of meerschaums began to fashion their pipes after the briars.

During World War I, briar pipes became popular among soldiers in the field, and the soldiers carried their desire for these pipes home—through Europe and to the United States. Cigarettes and cigars became generally popular in the 1920s, largely because they could be smoked easily almost anywhere. If it had not been for briar, the pipe-smoking industry might have died. No other pipes were as convenient to smoke.

Today the briar pipe is the most popular by far. Excellent briar pipes not only smoke sweetly and are durable, but also possess a beauty of grain and richness in color that cannot be surpassed even by well-seasoned meerschaums. Master-crafted briar freehands (pipes shaped entirely by hand) are as exquisite in their fluid lines as any of the most intricately carved meerschaum pipes.

It is only the burl, the knotty section that forms above the root of the heath tree, *Erica arborea*, that serves the pipemaker. The plant is one of several hundred species of *Erica* that grow largely in South Africa and the Mediterranean regions. Briar, the best of which is found along the arid, rocky coasts of the Mediterranean, is harvested primarily in Spain, southern France, Corsica, Sardinia, Al-

bania, Dalmatia, Greece, and Algeria. The wood from any of these areas can be excellent. When one type or another has been lauded by particular pipe companies, it generally has been done for advertising purposes alone.

Lying just below the surface of the ground, the burl of the plant is a section that acts as an anchor for the main roots and trunk which stem from it. The burl also is a storehouse for the sap that is needed to preserve the plant during the long dry season. As the plant develops, the burl increases in size, expanding the root-canal system which brings water to the plant. The larger and older the plant, the larger the burl.

Burls that are congested with root canals produce finely grained wood. Plants that develop on rocky hills and must survive extremes of weather normally produce the best and most closely grained wood for pipes. Plants growing in the lush lower regions receive a more consistent quantity of moisture, flourish, and produce a great deal of foliage, but their burls do not become as large or as dense as those of hill plants. And young wood, no matter where it is grown, is never very densely grained.

The best wood grows in the most remote districts and costs more to harvest than lesser grades because it must be carried out on pack animals. More than geography or topography, time contributes toward the scarcity of excellent briar. It takes fifty or a hundred

Knights errant on a masterfully carved briar, c. 1850. Note detail in the figures of the horses, the splintered lances, the proud face of the victor—all set off by the mellow color of the burl of natural briar on which this rare pipe rests.

Solace of a pipe in war is caught by Winslow Homer in Civil War sketches (above r.) and painting (r.), "The Briarwood Pipe," in which a Zouave smoking long-stemmed briar watches a friend whittling a pipe. Above l.: Jan Sobieski, 17th-century Polish soldier-king, graces 200-year-old wooden pipe.

years of growth to produce a prime burl. A prime burl is one large enough to contain enough hard briar to produce at least thirty or forty blocks when the soft, grainless wood that has grown into the burl is cut away. Since many areas where top briar was harvested long ago are exhausted now, new lands are gradually being opened. Today the main supplier of prime briar wood is Greece.

The briar is brought to the marketplace by wood merchants who contract to har-

vest certain tracts. In harvesting a new area, the first step is to set up a convenient, centrally located mill for sawing and processing. Natives dig around and under each burl, then saw off the roots and the foliage above ground, leaving a small portion of the trunk to prevent the core of the burl from drying out too rapidly. The harvested burls are carried to the mill site, where they are buried in shallow trenches to allow them to dry slowly. If the burls dry too rapidly, they begin to crack and

Left: Wilke briars include several in-house designs. From l. to r.: "Papa" shape, one with square-cut bowl, a rough-edged freehand, and two standards—a half-bent tipped Dublin and a straight billiard with saddle stem. Above: Napoleon in briar.

117

are useless for manufacturing. After they have dried sufficiently to be safely processed, they are uncovered, washed, and scrubbed clean, then placed in water and boiled to remove the inner sap slowly.

At the sawmills the burls are cut in one of two ways: either into blocks which conform in size and shape to specifications of an international grading system, or into "plateau" blocks. The plateau is a block of straight-grained wood cut from the best (or outer) portions of the burl with the gnarled surface left on. The rough-topped Danish freehand pipes are beautiful examples of the fullest exploitation of this type of wood. Almost all excellent freehand straight-grain pipes are cut from this type of block.

After being cut into blocks, the briar is allowed to dry slowly for about a year. During this time, great care is taken to dry the wood evenly. If the outer portions dry faster than those within, tension is placed on the block which may ultimately crack it. After seasoning, the blocks are separated according to their shapes and sizes, loaded into sacks, and shipped. When a manufacturer receives his sacks of fresh briar blocks, he sorts them according to size and shape and stores them in bins. There they are allowed to dry even more thoroughly.

Since a pipe turned from a block that is partially moist might easily warp, pipe manufacturers are very careful to use only ex-

118

tremely dry blocks. Today's manufacturers pay more attention to this than did their counterparts in years gone by when seasoning of wood prior to manufacturing was not so thorough. Then the smoker had to season a briar pipe by smoking it very slowly at first to force out whatever sap remained and to keep it from cracking. Sap gave the smoke a very "green" taste. Briar pipes made by the finer companies today are seasoned so thoroughly they are "broken in" before they reach the smoker.

Manufacturing of briar pipes falls into two categories. Production of the standard shapes—apple, billiard, Dublin, pot, pear, and prince—provides the heaviest workload for most factories. Many major manufacturers of fine pipes also produce a limited line of excellent freehand pipes, no two of which are alike. In each factory, these freehands are created only by a top few pipemakers and only when exceptionally fine briar is available. (In the past few years certain Danish companies such as Praben Hølm, Nørding, and Knute have been producing only freehands.)

In the first step of manufacture for standard shapes, the blocks are trimmed on the sides. The prepared blocks are then put on press-like machines which cut out rough bowls about halfway down the blocks to just above where the shank will come into the bowl. These machines also bore out the inner bowl, or "tobacco hole."

On a woodworking lathe with specially adapted cutters, a technician of the Arlington Briar Corporation roughly shapes the interior and exterior of a bowl in one step. Rough-cut briars lie in trough in foreground.

Pipe body is formed on a "frazing"
machine (top l.), with a template, or pipe
pattern, guiding the cutter to reproduce
a chosen shape. Above l.: A bowl is routed.
Above r.: Shank hole is drilled for snug-fitting
stem. Right: Sanding and buffing pipes.

The next step is to rough in the shank. The block is put on a frazing machine which cuts each pipe the same because the cutting blade is governed by a metal pipe pattern. The workman merely traces the pattern and a high-speed cutting blade rounds off the bottom of the bowl and cuts out a rough, oversized shank. After the bowls, or "stummels," are turned, the channel and mortise are bored and the butt of the shank is squared off.

In the sanding department of the factory, rough edges are taken off the pipes while extreme care is taken to avoid sanding the butt of the shank. Any rounding from the sanding wheel would prevent the already squared off shank from fitting flush with the bit. (Bits or stems are made either from premolded vulcanite or occasionally are hand-cut from solid rods of vulcanite or acrylic plastic.) The bit is fitted to the shank, then both are sanded down until they fit flush, and the hand sanding continues until the finish of the pipe is smooth. The factory's experienced pipe men usually work in this department because more skill is required to hand-shape the final dimensions of the bowls.

After sanding, the smooth bowls are graded according to the quality of the wood and workmanship. All the pipes are destined to become either "firsts" or "seconds." Firsts are flawless pipes; seconds are those with pits, fissures, and fills.

The pipes are divided further into several groups according to grade of wood. The most highly valued pipes are the straight grains. In these, the root canals run vertically on the bowl with a circular, or "bird's-eye," grain appearing at the top and bottom of the bowl and running along the upper and lower sides of the shank. The next most valuable pipe is the bird's-eye. A perfect bird's-eye pipe will have the circular end grain on the sides of the bowl and stem with straight grain running horizontally on the top and bottom of the shank, the top and bottom of the bowl, and the front and back of the bowl. The third type of graining is known as "bald" wood, as it has little visible grain. Briar of this type generally comes from an area of the burl where the soft wood of the trunk and roots has worked its way into the hard briar. Bald wood is avoided as much as possible because its poor smoking qualities reduce the value of even the best crafted pipes. Naturally, only a few pipes have a perfect straight or bird's-eye grain and, when these are densely grained, they bring the highest prices on the market. Most bowls, however, have a mixed graining.

Once the grader has divided the firsts from the seconds, he must determine the grades, or series, within each group according to the density of the grain. Regardless of the grain direction or pattern, certain woods are more densely grained than others; that is, the root canals are spaced more closely together. Because of their value and scarcity, fine, dense

Finishing touches to rank-and-file briars include pitting the surface of some (top) for a sandblasted look, and filling in imperfections (bottom l.). After staining and buffing, firm's name is stamped on the pipe (bottom r.).

straight-grain and bird's-eye bowls are set aside and kept until the factory has a selection. The straight grain is the scarcer of the two.

After grading, all the perfect bowls are sent to the staining department. Those pipes which are nicely grained but have small, superficial pits are sandblasted to remove the defects. This produces a very rough finish. They are then stained a dark or black stain. Some perfect bowls that are dense but not beautifully grained are sandblasted also.

Those pipes destined to be seconds are sent to the filling department where workers with small drills clean out pits and soft spots. The holes are then filled with putty. After the putty dries, the bowls are resanded or sandblasted, then stained. Seconds are graded in the same way as firsts.

After the pipes have been stained, emblems are put on the stems. Then the pipes are buffed with progressively finer grades of tripoli rock or unsewn, laminated cloth wheels to bring out the grain and produce a more lustrous finish. If the stem is to be bent, the pipe at this point is usually placed stem down in a bed of hot sand until the vulcanite or Lucite is pliable, then it is hand-bent and allowed to cool in the new shape. When this job is completed, the shanks are stamped with the company and/or series name and shape number. The final task in production is shining and polishing. The bowl is buffed using a wheel coated with carnauba wax which brings out the beauty of the grain and gives the pipe a finished look. (Some series, however, are left with a mat finish.) The stem is also buffed with a high-luster paste, after which the pipes are ready for boxing.

Certain manufacturers vary these procedures slightly, but the basic steps are the same. You will note that there is no mention of metal baffles or filters being inserted anywhere during manufacturing. The manufacturers of high-grade pipes do not use these gadgets, nor do they apply lacquer finishes.

The freehand pipe is the most beautiful and expensive of all briar pipes. Rather than being cut from blocks by machine as are the standard shapes, freehands are designed by hand by the most highly skilled craftsmen in the factory from slabs of plateau wood. The pipemaker's first step in creating a freehand is to sand and polish the slab in order to examine the grain closely. Then he sketches a design on the wood and roughly cuts out the pipe using a band or hack saw. After the tobacco hole, mortise, and draft hole are drilled, the rough bowl is filed and chiseled by hand to a shape very close to the final one.

This operation is followed by sanding the bowl both on a machine and by hand until it is smooth. If superficial pits appear, the shape generally is creatively altered by sanding to remove them, or a design is tooled over them. Before the pipes are stained, they are carefully graded and those which need small

A Perfect Blend: Fruit, cheese, wine, and a pipeful in a Wilke freehand —an aristocratic briar in its natural state. Buffed to a fine finish, Wilke pipes are otherwise untreated, in keeping with firm's century-old tradition.

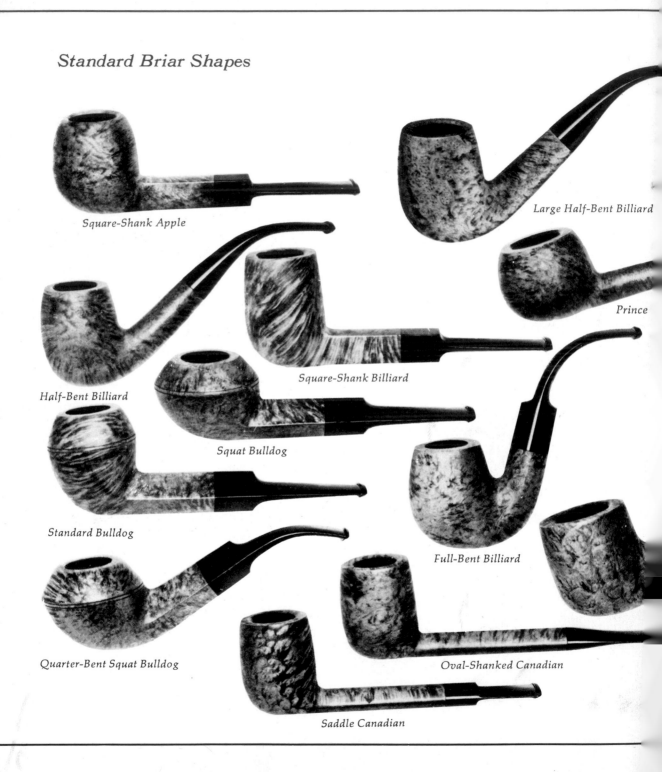

Standard Briar Shapes

Square-Shank Apple

Large Half-Bent Billiard

Half-Bent Billiard

Square-Shank Billiard

Prince

Squat Bulldog

Standard Bulldog

Full-Bent Billiard

Quarter-Bent Squat Bulldog

Oval-Shanked Canadian

Saddle Canadian

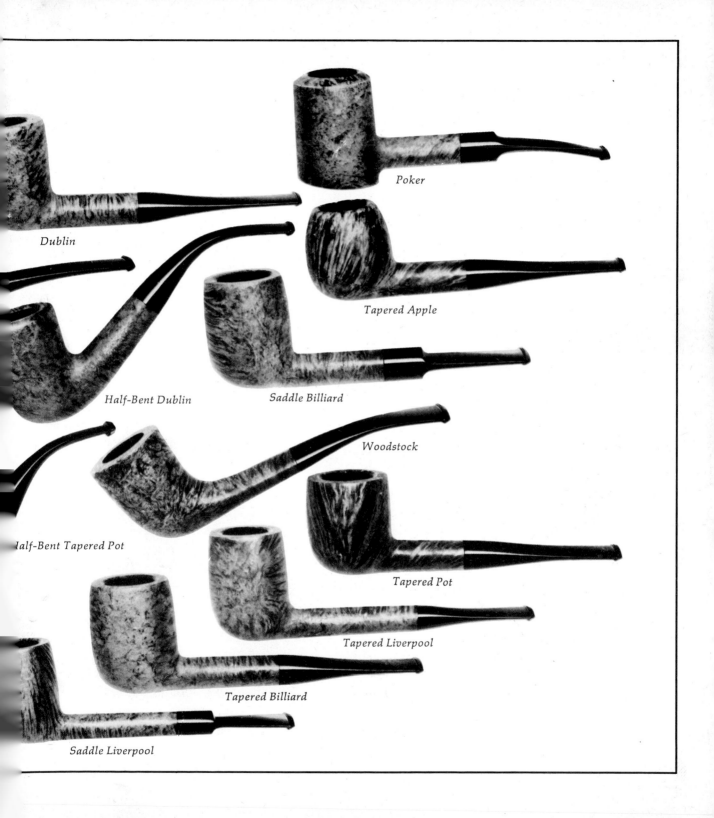

Poker

Dublin

Tapered Apple

Half-Bent Dublin

Saddle Billiard

Woodstock

Half-Bent Tapered Pot

Tapered Pot

Tapered Liverpool

Tapered Billiard

Saddle Liverpool

fills or have a less-than-beautiful grain are sandblasted. Grading is basically the same with the smooth, straight-grained freehands as it is with the standard shapes: the denser or tighter the graining, the more valuable the pipe.

In the case of Danish freehands, one may find a few small pits or tiny fills in the least expensive pipes; yet, these superficial flaws in no way affect the smoke and are almost impossible to detect by the amateur. Fills and pits do not affect the smoke unless they are large and located on the pipe where they weaken it.

When selecting briar pipes, quality of wood and workmanship and the type of graining are the prime considerations. As with meerschaum, the larger and more intricately designed pipes usually are more expensive and the smaller, plainer designs cost less, but the graining of the wood is the determining factor. Pipes made of dense, straight-grained wood are by far the most expensive. They are beautiful and generally they are lighter in weight than similar shapes made of younger or poorly grained wood. They have a tendency to absorb moisture much more slowly, which means they will smoke more sweetly and need to be rested less often. A straight grain takes a little longer than some pipes to reach its peak flavor but after a few days of smoking it holds a high level of flavor indefinitely, even under very heavy smoking, provided it is cleaned regu-

larly to remove tars and oils. The bird's-eye, or end, grain at the bottom of the bowl of a straight-grain pipe absorbs moisture more quickly than other grains. Yet, because of its position, it allows the moisture to drain away from the tobacco and the channel, thus keeping the smoke dry.

Bird's-eye grain is not so scarce as the straight grain; yet pipes which possess this type of graining and which are very dense as well are not plentiful since they also are from old, prime burls. High-quality bird's-eye pipes are as light as straight grains and they color faster because the more absorbent end grain faces the burning area. For this same reason, bird's-eye pipes cannot be smoked as long nor as hard as straight grains without a rest.

Bald, or grainless, wood is not desirable because it is soft and more prone to burn out than the other types. It becomes saturated by moisture more quickly than grains of fine briars and therefore needs more frequent rests. On occasion, it fills up with tars to such an extent that it remains sour even after drying. High-grade pipes will have little of this grainless wood in them. Those that do are generally at the inexpensive end of the first-grade lines or, more often, in the category of seconds. A small amount of bald wood will not seriously affect the smoke. It simply is not very attractive.

Few pipes are perfect examples of any of these basic types of grain. They are

Savinelli briars: "Autograph" model in center is individually handcrafted from aged Sardinian briar, the stem made of hand-cut vulcanite. Two "Nonpareils"—smooth with horn shank (l.) and sandblasted (r.)—complete the array.

generally a mixture of types varying in degrees of density. In most cases one will find that a dense piece of briar after a period of time will prove superior to the pipe made of younger wood, or of wood coming from a mixed part of the burl.

In selecting a briar pipe, a smoker should buy the best he can afford. The finer pipes, in addition to offering beauty and performance, will, with proper care, last him a lifetime. Standard firsts, excluding straight grains, generally range in price from $12.50 to $45. If a smoker spends more than $45 for this type of pipe, he is paying for a brand name, not for the quality of the wood. Straight-grain standards, when they are available, run between $50 and $75. To spend more than that would be to make a mistake, even for a pipe of an extra large size.

Standard sandblast or relief-finish pipes produced by reputable manufacturers are excellent for those who want a pipe for sport or work instead of a smoothly finished pipe which might be scarred. The smoker should not assume, however, that this sort of finish will smoke noticeably cooler. The ability of a roughly finished pipe to disperse heat compared with that of a smoothly finished pipe of the same shape is negligible. If the woods are of the same grade, the sandblast type might be slightly lighter because some of the wood has been removed to produce the finish.

Pipes of this type with medium-sized, or even large and extra-large bowls, generally run between $11 and $40. Frankly, I must admit that some $40 pipes finished in this manner smoke no better than a few I have owned that cost about $20. They are all well-crafted pipes. If you see one costing more than $40, put it down.

Generally, a second will be offered under a series name and the manufacturer will be identified only on the box, never on the pipe itself. These pipes run from $6 to $15, but one should think twice about paying the higher amounts. You can buy beautiful firsts for the same price.

Pipes at the inexpensive end of the line generally have a number of fills and bald wood. Nonetheless they are excellent pipes for the beginner or for smoking at work. Count on these pipes to require a long rest after hard smoking. Seconds costing from $8.50 to $10 will be made of better wood and, occasionally, the smoker may chance to find one that is quite nice. In some cases the higher priced second will perform as well as some "firsts." If the smoker is not concerned about a few small fills, he can save money by buying seconds. However, always be concerned with the density of the wood.

Freehands are the jewels of the pipe-making trade and are priced from $25 to as much as $2,000. Quite often rather large, these pipes are made from very old, prime, straight-grained plateau wood, cut and styled by hand.

The Danish freehands generally display the naturally rough surface of the burl on the top of the bowl, while English companies normally produce freehands with smooth or carved tops. The very best of these pipes start at about $50 for a sandblast finish. Some are offered for less; however, they generally are not made of such dense wood as the more expensive grades. Those in the upper grades are beautifully grained. Charatan, GBD, Savinelli, and Nørding make some of the finest specimens. The lower priced freehands, most of them made by Danish manufacturers, are plentiful today. The finest grades, priced higher than $60, are rather scarce, however.

The coloring of a new pipe is generally a reliable indication of its quality. Pipes that are very lightly stained or not stained at all are inviting the smoker to examine their grain. The finest briar pipes are always light in color. When a manufacturer puts a dark stain on a pipe, he is often trying to obscure an unattractive graining pattern. Those who prefer pipes with dark finishes should remember that a light-colored pipe grows darker and richer as it is smoked. The final gloss that is applied to a pipe by the manufacturer is another clue to quality. Quality manufacturers use only wax, which does not seal the grain. Varnishes and shellacs are used on lower quality items to set the stain that has been applied to the bowl; if it should bleed off when the pipe is smoked, an ugly piece of wood would be left exposed.

Smokers who have smoked fine pipes will, with rare exceptions, insist that no metal baffles or filters be used in their pipes. Why? There simply is no need for such gadgets in fine pipes. A metal piece constricts the smoke coming through the channel and increases condensation which ultimately is held in the shank, causing the pipe to sour faster. It's also a nuisance. Cleaning the pipe after a smoke without removing the stem becomes impossible when there is a mortise and tenon fitting. A pipe that is uncluttered through the shank and stem smokes drier and more flavorfully, and is easier to care for.

Ever since I began to smoke a pipe, I have heard many fanciful notions about how to get the most out of smoking. Some men are convinced they should smear all kinds of substances in the bowls of their new pipes. Others say that to break in a pipe properly you must smoke little pinches of tobacco at first and increase the amount every full moon until the bowl is ready for regular use. Almost all, at one time or another, try some kind of filter, contraption, or miracle blend of tobacco. They fill their bowls, then use the probes on their pipe tools to gouge holes in the tobacco, rather than learning how to fill their bowls properly. All of this they do to get a sweet smoke, but they seldom are happy with what they receive. If the pipe smoker has patience enough to try quality pipes and tobaccos, and at the same time use reasonable smoking techniques and

habits, he will find that pipes do not have to bite, burn, or smell foul, but actually are instruments of enjoyment.

Certain manufacturers, particularly in the United States, have capitalized on the ignorance of smokers. Rather than try to educate their potential customers and supply them with high-quality products, they have produced a multitude of gimmicks. Pipes made from metal and low-grade briar simply cannot in any way compare with the simple designs of high-grade pipes made from excellent, well-seasoned prime burls. One company even goes so far as to guarantee that its specially filtered briar pipes will never, never become sour. I have never seen a briar pipe with moisture running through the shank that will not need a rest. Some tobacco manufacturers produce brands that are cut nearly as fine as cigarette tobacco so they stay lit no matter how poor the smoking habits of the smoker. They should perhaps include an asbestos tongue cover as a free gift with every can.

Only when the smoker begins selecting suitable tobaccos and pipes, properly cares for his pipe, and develops proper smoking habits will he begin to savor pipe smoking. Only then will his pipes stay lit and smoke sweetly while remaining cool and dry.

The following are the major producers of the finest briar pipes: Barling, BBB, Comoy, Charatan, Dunhill, GBD, Hilson, Jobey, Larsen, Peterson, Sasieni, Savinelli, and Stanwell produce a variety of pipes; Celius, Karl Erick, Knute, Nørding, and Ben Wade produce freehands exclusively. Also, do not overlook the fine hand-made pipes that are made by a few individual pipemakers in the United States.

Selection of Pipes

The selection of every smoking pipe should be made carefully. In that way the smoker will build a collection which, regardless of its size, does not include pipes that are not smoked. As a result he will avoid oversmoking and the consequent destruction of his favorite three or four pipes.

When selecting a pipe, the smoker should evaluate each on the basis of the following points: the pipe's appearance and style, its inner bowl design and size, the quality of material and craftsmanship, the pipe's comfort both in mouth and hand.

To the new smoker this may seem to be a complex procedure, but after gaining some experience he will be able to tell at a glance whether a pipe will perform well for him. However, even though two pipes may be identical in shape and design and even selected from the same grade of wood or the same series from a single manufacturer, there probably will be slight differences in taste from one pipe to another. No two pieces of wood are exactly alike structurally and, consequently, each one will season differently. Even

134

Preceding pages: Charatan briars include straight-grained freehand Supremes cut from plateau briar, and standard shapes cut from briar blocks. All display English craftsmanship that has maintained the firm's reputation for high standards since its founding in 1863.

though a smoker puts a good deal of effort into analyzing pipes before buying one, he still must make some allowance for the quirks of nature.

The first step in buying a pipe is to look over the selection of pipes your tobacconist carries and choose for closer examination several types which strike your fancy for some reason—shape, style, finish, stem. If one buys a pipe that doesn't appeal to him visually, it will end up collecting dust in some forgotten corner or will be given away.

Now consider the size of the pipe—both the capacity of the bowl and the over-all size—and the design of the inner bowl. Regardless of the number of different pipe shapes, the inner bowl of all pipes is limited to a number of basic sizes and designs, which affect the burning characteristics of the tobacco smoked in them. Most pipes (all briar-root and meerschaum pipes) are manufactured in a variety of sizes and inner-bowl designs. It is up to the smoker, after he has gained a little experience, to decide what sizes and designs conform best to his smoking habits. The smoker will notice a difference in the burning quality of the tobacco when he smokes a new pipe—in the ease with which he is able to smoke and the quality of the taste he experiences. It would be very difficult, indeed almost impossible, to designate a particular bowl size and design for a smoker without being able to talk to him, to become acquainted with his traits and preferences. The smoker should be aware that size and design weigh heavily on his ability to enjoy any given pipe.

The basic inner bowl designs are the conical, with tapered sides; the parallel, with parallel or slightly tapered sides; and the wide parallel, also called pots. These are available in a variety of sizes. There are two points to remember here. First, as the diameter of the inner bowl narrows, the tobacco tends to burn faster and with more heat. As the bowl widens, the tobacco tends to burn more slowly. Therefore it is generally true that the more aggressive a smoker is, the wider the bowl of his pipe should be.

The second point concerns the capacity of the inner bowl. Smokers may develop idiosyncratic smoking patterns and appetites which are not always in keeping with their personal stature. For instance, you may find a large man who enjoys a petite pipe. Because each design is available in several sizes the smoker has the opportunity to choose a pipe that not only is properly designed for his smoking habits, but also has an ideal capacity for the length of smoke he enjoys. The smoker will find a variety of outer bowl designs that smoke similarly to one another, because the inner designs are much the same. It is only when the smoker makes a radical change to a pipe of much larger or smaller inner bowl capacity, or from a wide inner bowl to a narrow one, or vice versa, that there will be a notice-

able difference in the smoking quality of his pipes. There are no hard and fast rules concerning design and size because these factors relate to individual tastes. Choose a pipe according to your taste and habits rather than following arbitrary rules about what is "right."

Experience is the smoker's best teacher. After he has several pipes (providing they have been taken care of so they all perform in the manner intended), he will find that certain shapes seem to smoke better than others. When he adds further to his collection, he should concentrate on buying pipes whose inner-bowl size and design come close to those of the pipes he enjoys most. The novice should begin with pipes with medium-sized bowls. If he finds after a few months that he is unable to smoke as much tobacco as that size bowl holds, he should experiment with pipes that have smaller bowls. If, on the other hand, he finds his pipes are smoking too hot and wet (assuming this is not a result of poor smoking habits or bad tobacco selection), he should try a wider bowl at first, then, if that does not clear up the problem, one both wider and larger. Smokers should avoid selecting pipes just for variety of shape. They should stay with shapes that have the capacity and inner-bowl designs that suit their smoking habits. Even with these limitations, there will be many different pipes from which to choose.

Whether a bowl has a thin or thick wall has little bearing on the quality of smoke that comes through the mouthpiece. A thin-walled pipe naturally will heat up faster and be warmer to the touch because there is less material for heat to radiate through. On the other hand, a pipe with a thick wall generally is heavier in weight and somewhat less comfortable in the mouth.

After the smoker has determined which pipes are both attractive and well designed for his needs, he should examine them to make sure the quality of material used justifies the price and that the pipe has no defects as far as workmanship is concerned, such as draft holes bored too deeply or off-center, or a stem that doesn't fit well.

The final point to be observed is how comfortable the pipe will be in your mouth or in your hand. If a pipe is uncomfortable, all of its technical and aesthetic qualities will mean very little to you. Important questions to ask are: Where will I be smoking and what activities will I be performing? A smaller, lighter pipe is ideal for smoking at work. It rests in the mouth comfortably for a long time. Pipes with bent stems which put less leverage on the jaw and teeth also are very good for the active smoker. The heavy, large bowl is best for smoking at home when you are seated and have a hand free to hold the pipe.

A final thought: When you select pipes of different materials, try not to compare them too precisely. Rather, judge them on their own merits.

Clockwise, starting with white Dutch porcelain with Bakelite stem: Two English briars in bulldog and poker shapes, three handcrafted Danish briars, topmost with horn shank, Belgian plastic with pressed meerschaum lining, and half-bent French briar of Algerian burl.

Part Three

Tobacco:
"The Special Herb"

Tobacco, the "special herb" Columbus noted in the Indies, becomes a source of pleasure only after careful implementation of relatively complex growing and processing procedures. Perhaps no other leaf is so dependent upon the nurturing of variable properties of structure, color, and chemical composition for its final commercial value. In fact, the species of tobacco found in almost all commercial blends, *Nicotiana tabacum*, is evidently unable to thrive without cultivation.

Since its discovery by Europeans, there have been attempts to improve techniques of cultivating and curing tobacco. Hernán Cortés was probably the first European to observe the tobacco industry, albeit in a primitive form. He saw how Aztecs, who had inherited knowledge of tobacco from the Mayans, grew the plant and sold dried leaves in the market. As early Spanish planters expanded their growing areas in the New World, they quickly learned about cultivation and became adept at developing seed beds, transplanting young plants, and removing suckers for maximum yield. A beautiful, sweet leaf was their reward.

Many nations were anxious to profit from the cultivation of tobacco and heralded planters' discoveries that this curious plant would adapt to varying soils and flourish in countries far removed from the Western Hemisphere. Today tobacco is grown as far north as central Sweden and as far south as New Zealand. In adapting to strange soils and climatic conditions, the character of the proliferating tobacco was changed to such an extent that it confused botanists who were trying to pinpoint its origin and led erroneously to the classification of several new species. For years people believed tobacco originated in Africa or Asia and could not be persuaded that it was indigenous to the New World. But it is, and the main production of tobacco for world trade has remained in the Western Hemisphere, which

Preceding pages: North Carolina farmers harvesting a field of tobacco for flue-curing. Worker (rear r.) places leaves in bulk-curing rack of tractor-drawn harvester as they are primed. Right: English trade card, c. 1726. Earliest English symbol of American tobacco was a black Indian with pipe and leaves.

produces one-third of the world's supply.

Tobacco Is Refined

By studying progress in the American tobacco industry, we are able to understand changes in the cultivation and processing of tobaccos in general. This is not meant to demean European tobaccos or those which are, after long development from the original seed, peculiar to other lands, but it is a fact that their importance has steadily diminished as the American types have become predominant.

Though the tobaccos familiar to us have changed considerably since the original cultivation by the Portuguese and Spanish, they now seem somewhat more stable and should not soon undergo again any radical changes in plant type. Further, it is unlikely that the refined growing and curing techniques now employed will be altered significantly in the near future.

Today's tobacco is of much higher quality than that produced when the industry was young. Today "Virginia" tobacco is a brightly colored, light-bodied leaf; the tobacco harvested in early Tidewater Virginia was dark in color and strong in taste. The alteration in appearance and mildness is due to several factors. The strain of tobacco is different, growing techniques have gradually improved, and, most importantly, progress has been made in methods of curing the leaf.

Though John Rolfe's tobacco grown in Jamestown from imported Spanish seed was hailed by London merchants as "Oronoko," their name for the sweet leaf produced by the Spanish, they soon recognized two kinds of tobacco on the market—Virginian and Spanish. The *Nicotiana tabacum* grown in Virginia was a vast improvement over the bitter native *N. rustica,* but the soil and climate of the Tidewater produced a tobacco different from that of the Latin American plantations, from which the seed came. Later, as settlers moving northward about 1631 took seeds from the "tobacconized colony" with them, even the difference

141

*Tobacco ripe for harvesting (above)
has horn-worm markings not uncommon in
cultivated leaf. Slight damage
does not lessen the value of the crop.
Right: Farmer and his wife gather sticks of
looped tobacco bound for curing barn.*

between Virginia and Maryland growing conditions was sufficient to produce alterations in product. Tobacco is extremely sensitive to any difference in soil and subsoil, climate, and method of curing. That is why a grower in one geographical area cannot change to a type of seed grown elsewhere and produce a leaf true to that seed. The long evolution of tobacco production has led to a highly localized and specialized industry, with each area producing certain types and grades especially suited to the manufacture of one or more definite tobacco products.

Some processes are common to all tobaccos: seeding, transplanting, curing in some type of barn. The colonists sowed seeds in boxed seed beds, as they were accustomed to do with cabbage, and in May the young plants were transplanted to mounds about four feet apart. All tobacco seeds are still sown in either hot beds or cold frames.

One ounce of seed contains about 300,000 to 350,000 individual seeds. A tablespoonful is adequate to sow one hundred square yards of seed bed. This ultimately provides enough seedlings to plant three to five acres. An acre produces one to two thousand pounds of fresh tobacco leaves, depending on the type. However, all tobaccos ripened in the field contain about eighty percent moisture; curing reduces this to twenty to twenty-five percent. Thus five hundred pounds of fresh leaf yield only about one hundred pounds of

tobacco after it is cured.

Tobacco seeds begin to germinate at about 65 degrees Fahrenheit. After the seedlings reach six to eight inches, they are transplanted to the fields, either by machinery or by hand. Transplanting usually takes place from late March to early June, depending on the location of the growing area.

In the early 1600s farmers learned that by topping each growing plant—cutting off the flowering head and pruning each stalk to ten or twelve leaves—and by suckering—removing the secondary shoots that spring forth after the major leaves are grown—the leaves that remained developed much better. This is still standard procedure. When it ripens, tobacco is harvested by stalk cutting, in which the entire mature plant is cut down, or by priming, a method by which the leaves are picked from the stalk as they ripen.

Tobacco classification is complex and varies in terminology, but the standards outlined by the U.S. Department of Agriculture list pipe tobaccos in terms of curing method: flue-cured, fire-cured, air-cured, plus miscellaneous (*N. rustica*, Perique, and Eastern Ohio Export).

The first method of curing was by air. Early accounts of Indians of various regions of America tell of air-drying, either in the shade of huts or in the sun. There are descriptions of Lake Huron Indians using this class of tobacco in a rather sophisticated barter

Farmer moves a bulk-curing rack of tobacco from harvester into barn for flue-curing. Bulk-curing is a relatively new method in which process of looping tobacco onto sticks is eliminated.

146

"Outside the Curing Barn," by Thomas Hart Benton, was part of a massive advertising campaign conducted in 1940s by the American Tobacco Company. Talents of American artists were enlisted for a series of promotional paintings.

system with other tribes. The French explorer Jacques Cartier gave a comprehensive account of the use of tobacco in those northern parts in the sixteenth century: "There groweth also a certain kind of herbe, whereof in summer they make great provision for all the yeere, making great account of it, and first they cause it to be dried, in the sunne, then weare it about their neckes wrapped in a little beasts skinne made like a little bagge. . . ."

Processing techniques in the colonies evolved slowly. Harvesting was primitive; picked leaves were piled in heaps to dry. By 1610, rather than picking individual leaves, growers had begun to cut the entire plant after it had ripened. In 1617 one George Lambert discovered tobacco cured better when hung.

After the tobacco was fully dried, or cured, and when the humidity was high enough to make the dried leaves supple, the leaves were stripped from the stalks. In the 1700s the next step was "bulking," a process by which all the leaves were pushed together in one area to undergo a "sweat"—a mild fermentation of the tobacco which is the beginning of the aging process. Aging is still a vital part of tobacco production. It removes rawness and gum, mellows the leaf, and allows aroma to develop. Freshly cured tobacco has a flat, almost unpleasant herbal odor. Finally, early Virginia tobacco growers packed the leaves in wooden casks—hogsheads—using lever presses. The hogsheads were stored so the leaves could age and mellow further.

Curing as practiced by the fledgling tobacco industry of the 1600s was simply a cruder version of the air-curing method of today. Curing tobaccos by air is a method of depleting tobacco leaves on the stalk of excess plant food created during ripening. Air-curing generally takes place in simple wooden barns constructed of narrow boards arranged vertically and fixed with hinges so they can be opened for ventilation.

The stalks, speared on sticks, are hung across tier poles inside the barns on three or four different levels, spaced so that air can reach all parts of the plants. This drying process takes a month or two, depending on the weather. If conditions are exceptionally moist or cold during this period of curing, growers occasionally shut the vents and supply some type of heat to hasten the curing.

Curing is completed when the central rib of each leaf is seen to be free of plant fluids. After the curing, the plants are allowed to remain in the barns until the dry leaves have absorbed enough moisture from the air to make them pliable. When the leaves are removed from the stalks, they are sorted into several grades according to their positions up from the base of the stalk.

Curing methods used in Virginia spread to Maryland as tobacco planters moved there. The Maryland leaf was a variation on the Virginian, due to the difference in soil and climate, but it was because of politics that tobacco production in Maryland took a different turn. Virginia, ruled by a direct representative of the British crown, was compelled to ship her tobacco directly to England where it was then re-exported to the continent, to the great profit of England. Because Maryland had certain sovereign rights, she was able to export tobacco directly to France and the Netherlands. Thus from the beginning Maryland's tobacco industry was aimed at the rapidly expanding continental market.

At the close of the eighteenth century, Virginia and Maryland accounted for about eighty percent of all leaf grown in the United States. The spread of tobacco to southern Ohio, Kentucky, Tennessee, and Missouri brought changes. A significant one was the adaptation of the basic Virginia seed to the soil of the new areas, where all tobaccos became known as Burley. Presumably this name came from one of the more affluent planters in the new tobacco-growing region. The Burley plants were dark and heavy compared with the parent Virginia tobaccos, which were becoming milder and more refined.

During the 1800s, the curing techniques of American tobaccos developed rapidly. Utilization of fire, and eventually charcoal, resulted in a speedier process and a different quality of product. Colonial growers had found that the fires sometimes needed to protect uncured leaves from dampness not

Harvested tobacco hangs looped on sticks in a conventional curing barn for flue-curing. Heat is applied slowly to begin color change. Later the temperature is raised to fix the color and dry out stems.

only warded off disease and preserved tobacco shipped abroad, but also imparted a certain finish and aroma to the tobacco. As buyers responded favorably to these qualities, fire-curing became the general practice in various parts of Virginia.

Fire-cured tobaccos are harvested by the stalk-cutting method and cured in barns similar to air-curing barns, except that they are sealed more tightly to maximize the smoke. The leaf is allowed to yellow naturally for several days without the use of heat. Then slow-burning fires of hardwood logs or sawdust are burned in the barn until the leaf is completely yellowed. Such gradual, even curing avoids loss of the tobacco's natural oils. The temperature of the fires is increased and held at a high point until the leaf is completely dry.

Fire-cured tobaccos grown today in central Virginia and extreme southwestern and northwestern Tennessee resemble the tobaccos from which they originate. These heavy, smoky-flavored tobaccos dominated the industry in the eighteenth and nineteenth centuries, not only in Virginia, Maryland, and the Carolinas, but also in most of the western area, including Missouri, which now produces White Burley.

Smokers' tastes in those times were not terribly refined. Fire-cured tobaccos were used predominantly in the manufacture of plug tobaccos (the flat plug, popular in the East, and the thick, western plug), rolls, and twists. All of these were sweetened in varying degrees. They could be sliced for smoking in a pipe, cut for a "chaw," or even grated for snuff.

With the emergence of the cigarette, which demands very light-bodied tobaccos, the market for these dark tobaccos diminished. Today the fire-cured industry's production amounts to only around two to three percent of America's total tobacco output. It is used principally in the manufacture of snuff in the United States, although some is used in chewing tobacco and in cheap, strong cigars. About half of this dark tobacco is exported to Africa and the West Indies. Fire-cured leaf is also produced in Malawi, Tanzania, Uganda, and Italy, mostly for local consumption. Lighter tobaccos are replacing this type of tobacco in other countries as they did in the United States in the 1880s.

Modern Tobaccos

The only commercial tobacco today which truly resembles the first tobaccos grown in the colonies of Virginia and Maryland is the dark air-cured type, with its heavy leaf. Like fire-cured tobacco, it does not play an important role in American production of pipe tobacco. Grown in areas adjacent to the fire-cured sections of Kentucky, Tennessee, and northern Virginia, its major use in the United States is in the manufacture of chewing tobacco. It is also

Before the start of an auction, a Federal inspector examines a hand of tobacco, grading each lot on warehouse floor. A U. S. standard grade guarantees the farmer a minimum price on each lot of his tobacco.

151

used to some degree in making cheap cigars, snuff, and inexpensive smoking mixtures.

Light air-cured tobaccos are an important factor in today's tobacco market. The two major types are White Burley and Maryland. White Burley was a mutation of the Burley leaf. All tobaccos grown in Kentucky, Tennessee, and Ohio were originally known as Burley; Twist Bud, Red Burley, and Little Burley became the principal types. It was not until the discovery of White Burley, however, (and the onset of the Civil War, which disrupted tobacco farming and trading in the Virginia-Maryland area) that a definite change in emphasis occurred in both the types of tobaccos and the areas in which production took place.

In 1864, George Webb, a tobacco grower in Brown County, Ohio, planted some seeds he had purchased in Bracken County, Kentucky. As they grew, he noticed they were a strange creamy color, quite unlike the green seedlings of Little Burley he had expected. Assuming that the seeds were bad and that the small plants were diseased, he destroyed what he had planted. The next year, because of a shortage of seed, he was forced to plant the remainder of the "failed" seeds. When the crop was harvested and shipped for sale, it was well received by buyers at the market. It was light-bodied, had a fine texture, and produced a milder smoke than the standard Burley tobaccos of the area.

The White Burley mutation was to become the only type of leaf grown as Burley. By 1875 it had become the most popular filler in plug tobaccos. As new products evolved, Burley became the base for most American smoking mixtures, as well as the principal constituent in American-made cigarettes, which it remains.

The taste of Burley is rather bland, mainly because it has very little sugar in its chemical composition, especially when compared with contemporary flue-cured Virginias, which have the highest sugar content of any tobacco. Burley used in pipe tobaccos is almost always flavored. The leaf has a good "drinking quality" (the ability to absorb large quantities of flavoring), as well as a fine texture and good burning quality.

Ever since its discovery, the popularity of White Burley has steadily grown. Today it is America's most popular tobacco. Its growing area, which includes Kentucky, Tennessee, western North Carolina, western Virginia, and parts of West Virginia, Ohio, Indiana, and Missouri, produces nearly thirty percent of the U.S. tobacco crop (600 million pounds annually). About ninety percent of the White Burley crop is used in the manufacture of smoking products in the United States. Burley is also grown in Canada, Italy, Spain, Japan, Mexico, certain central African nations, and Greece.

Production of Maryland tobacco has

Ignoring hurly-burly on the auction floor, a buyer (top l.) checks for that sweet smell of Virginia tobacco. Others (top r.) mill around, waiting for auction to begin, and offer their bids (bottom) as auction gets under way.

153

remained within the state, with the exception of a small area in eastern Ohio that had a short-lived success before changing to White Burley. Maryland tobacco amounts to only about two percent of the annual U.S. crop. It has never been popular in the United States; most of it is exported to Switzerland, Germany, and France, which have long preferred that type of leaf. In the past few years, however, it has gained somewhat in the U.S. because of its lightness and ability to add better burning qualities to American cigarettes. Besides that it is used to a limited degree as a cigar filler, and a few companies use it as a base in smoking mixtures, similar to the role given Burley.

Today's flue-cured tobacco was developed by Virginia and Carolina growers who had moved farther and farther into their states as the cultivation of tobacco exhausted the land. As they proceeded into the inland regions, they found the leaf becoming lighter in color. When the Civil War ended, soldiers who had sampled this lighter tobacco, taken from a small factory near Durham, North Carolina, carried the desire for it home with them—to the North and South. After the war, Virginia and North Carolina producers began growing this bright tobacco again and, by the beginning of the twentieth century, flue-cured tobacco dominated American production.

An accidental discovery in 1893 by a servant of Abisha Slade in Caswell County,

North Carolina, marked the beginning of the flue-curing process. This process eliminates the smoky flavor which results from open fires in curing barns and preserves the delicacy of the lighter leaf. The worker fell asleep while tending the curing of tobacco and the fires burned down. Trying to revive them in haste, he added charcoal to the fire. The tobacco became brighter and brighter. Luckily for the worker, and smokers thereafter, Mr. Slade recognized this change as an improvement.

The importance of this accident is not so much that fireless, smokeless heat was used, but that this type of heat was used on the particular bright tobaccos of Virginia and Carolina. Years before, crude flues had been used in Maryland, Ohio, and Missouri to experiment with curing but the tobaccos of those rich soils did not respond in the same way. Later, with the development of the flue-curing barn, that form of curing became predominant in Virginia and North Carolina.

Flue-curing begins immediately after the ripe leaves are brought from the field in order to minimize damage and spoilage. The process preserves the beautiful, bright-yellow leaf. Curing involves three phases: "yellowing," drying the leaf tissue and fixing the color, and drying the midrib of the leaf. During each step the temperature is raised to a progressively higher point and maintained there, until in the final step it reaches a maximum of 175 degrees Fahrenheit. Careful at-

Engraving of long-leaved N. tabacum *by Augsburg artist, Lukas Kilian, from 17th-century botanical work,* Hortus Eystettensis. *Unknown in Germany until 1556, plant was cultivated privately in garden of Bishop of Eichstaett.*

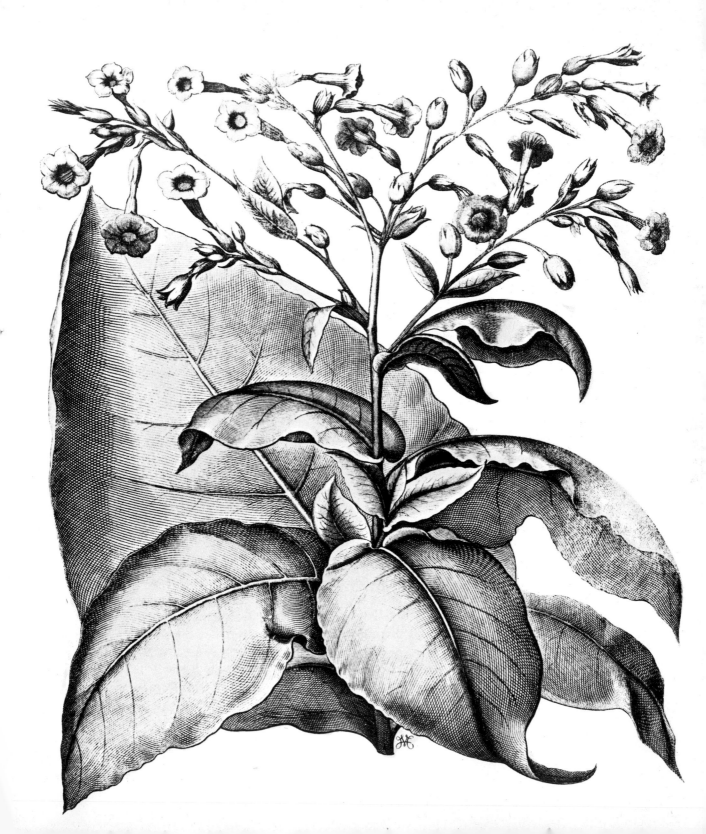

tention is paid to the condition of the leaf throughout the curing process; the tobacco could be ruined if heat were applied at the wrong stage. The entire process usually is completed in four to six days. The doors of the barn are then opened to allow the leaves to absorb moisture from the air.

Flue-cured tobacco leaves bear little resemblance to those which have been fire-cured. When the smoking qualities of the two are compared, the difference between them is even more noticeable. Flue-cured tobaccos are light-bodied with a subtle taste and aroma. Fire-cured tobaccos tend to be rather strong, lacking sweetness and delicacy of aroma.

"Virginia" flue-cured tobacco is grown in five belts in several states, each area's soil conditions affecting the color and body of the leaf. These belts produce this nation's largest annual crop, more than one billion pounds, twice the size of the Burley crop. About thirty to forty percent of the flue-cured crop is exported annually, making it America's largest export of a single type of tobacco. Worldwide, production of flue-cured tobacco amounts to about thirty-five percent of the total. Most of it is used in the manufacture of cigarettes.

American flue-cured tobacco is the highest quality available, with the exception of that grown in Rhodesia. Flue-cured tobaccos are also grown in China, the world's second largest producer, but little if any of the leaf grown there is exported. In addition they are grown in Japan, Canada, the Philippines, Thailand, Italy, Brazil, Argentina, Indonesia, Korea, Australia, New Zealand, India—the world's third largest producer—and elsewhere. A large percentage of the Indian and Rhodesian crops is purchased by England.

The development of modern methods in all areas of production, linked with mutations and some accidental discoveries which were recognized as improvements, has resulted in higher yields and finer leaf. As areas using air- and flue-curing methods were delineated, distinctions between types of tobaccos became apparent. By the late 1800s and early 1900s, the industry had evolved from the production of almost entirely dark tobaccos to production of a variety of types to please a variety of tastes. Changing market demands affected the quality and range of tobacco types grown and, in turn, this diversification altered methods of selling and marketing.

In 1842 the first loose-leaf auction was held in Richmond, Virginia. Before that, tobacco was sold in hogshead lots directly from farms or shipped on consignment to agents for sale. All hogsheads of tobacco were generally the same, though some distinction between Oronoko (grown predominantly in Maryland) and sweet-scented leaf was made. Waterlogged tobacco was thrown out, but adulterating tobacco with coal dust, cypress root, and other substances occurred regularly.

Earliest published illustration of Amerindians cultivating tobacco, which they used therapeutically, shows moistening, pressing, and drying small-leaved plants. Woodcut is from a French volume issued in 1630.

Americans also indulged in "nesting," hiding rotten or withered leaf under good, while in England tobacco for re-export would be weighed in lighter than it was upon arrival from America and heavier when shipped to the Continent. The consignment system and payment for tobacco in goods not available in the colonies became the curse of the planters. George Washington said that in four years out of five the tobacco he shipped to consignment merchants brought prices lower than those on the open market. The system of inherited debts was a peculiarity of the tobacco trade. These debts helped fan the fires of the Revolution, and the failure of Congress to arrange a debt settlement after the war contributed to the ruin of the aristocratic tobacco society of Virginia.

There was initially little interest in tobacco quality. But as European manufacturing practices improved, increasing competition (from the steadily improved Spanish leaf, for instance) depressed prices, and planters began to favor some system of inspection. Approved tobacco was bonded. There was a crude form of crop control—second growth (from sucker shoots) was banned and inferior grades of tobacco burned.

A decline in exports to Europe was paralleled by the first American tobacco manu-

Fig. 1.

Fig. 2.

Fig. 1.

Fig. 2.

facture. Begun in large seaports to service
sailors, significant manufacture developed relatively late. Only one tobacco factory is known
before 1750 and it required only sixty hogsheads a year. Before 1870 a factory product
was more or less a luxury. Cigars, when introduced, were an elite item, smoked in clubs and
by social leaders like the Adamses of Mas-
sachusetts. In 1830 one-fifth of the tobacco
crop went to U.S. factories; by 1860 about
one-half. Plugs for chewing were a major and
appropriately all-American product. Flavored
with rum, sugar, tonka beans from South
America, and spices, plugs were sliced and
used as pipe tobaccos, the first to be so treated.
By the end of the century, fierce competition
between manufacturers of plugs had begun
and brand names (in an incredible variety,
including such names as Darling Fanny Pan
Cake) became important for the first time.

When blends were introduced, the
business of tobacco buying became highly
specialized. As more and more factories were
opened, manufacturers became selective about
what they bought. Hogsheads were opened
and the contents auctioned off, at first by the
man who served as inspector. The heavy volume of manufacture in the Richmond area
eventually made opening hogsheads too time-
consuming and samples of loose leaf were
accepted for bidding.

After the Civil War the practice of
auctioning tobacco spread through the flue-

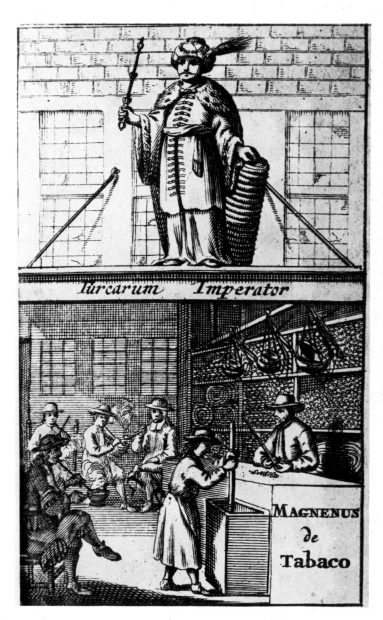

*Left: Engravings from Diderot's Encyclopedia
of 1791 show workers sorting and grading imported
tobaccos (top), while child at left in bottom picture selects
large leaves for wrappers; hummock of tobacco at
right is being humidified with sprinkled water.
Right: Turk marks Dutch tobacco shop of 1669.*

159

Faiseur de tabac.　　Ein Tabackmacher.

tabac en fleur, 1 die Tabacks Bluthe od: die Blume. 2 rouleau de tabac, 2 eine Rolle Taback. 3 regle.
as Tabackmaß. 4 pipe de tabac. 4 eine Pfeiffe Taback. 5 rouleau, 5 eine Rolle Knaster. 6 7 des feüilles
toutes sortes de tabac. 6 7 allerley Blätter als Türckische, Birginische, Zapffenberger, Engl. Holländische
ürnberger etc. 8 filer le tabac, 8 Taback Spinnen. 9 un roulleau, 9 eine Rolle Taback
n Priv. Maj.　　　　　　　　　　　　　　　　　　　　　　Martin Engelbrecht excud. A. V.

Une faiseuse de Tabac.　　Eine Tabackmacherin.

1. tabac de turquie en feüille, 1 Türckische Tabac-Blätter 2 tabac en fleur, 2 Tabacks-Blume. 3
3 das Tabackmaß. 4 feüille de tabac de turquie, 4 Türckische Tab. Blätter. 5 une tabatiere remplie, 5 ein
Tabacks Dosen 6 rouleau de tabac, 6 ein Taback Rolle. 7 pipe à fumer, 7 Tabacks pfeiffen. 8 toute sorte
en feüille, 8 allerley Tab. Blätter. 9 la presse, 9 die Taback Presse. 10 le devidon, 10 der Haspel
Cum Priv. Maj.　　　　　　　　　　　　　　　　　　　　　　Mart: Engelbrecht excu

curing belts, and in the early 1900s it was introduced to the Burley areas of Kentucky and Tennessee. The auction is the dominant form of sale today, although there is a limited hogshead market and some country sales and cooperative marketing. Over ninety percent of American leaf is sold at loose-leaf auctions, where each type of leaf is graded and certified by Government inspectors.

Before the manufacturing process can be begun, tobacco leaf must be cleaned, stemmed, and the moisture content reduced to prevent spoilage. Today most tobaccos (except Oriental and Latakia) are processed to produce "strips," large pieces of leaf with the stems removed. After the tobacco has been processed for aging it is packed in hogsheads under pressure and stored, sometimes for several years. During this period of aging, or fermentation, the tobacco undergoes chemical changes which reduce the nicotine and certain other substances in the leaf, resulting in a sweeter, mellower flavor. In the course of the process, the tobacco also darkens, just how much depending on the type.

Oriental tobaccos are present in most well-conceived luxury mixtures. While the experienced pipe smoker knows them well for the subtle flavor and aroma they impart, he probably has little or no knowledge of their origin.

Oriental tobaccos are grown in the picturesque area surrounding the northeastern Mediterranean, the Aegean, and most of the Black Sea. All these tobaccos became known as "Turkish" during the Ottoman Empire (1300-1918). Oriental tobaccos differ considerably from all other types—in chemical composition and in plant and leaf size—and have a subtle, yet rich, natural taste and aroma when properly cured. Their flavor and aroma are reminiscent of delicate spices and herbs. These differences make it difficult to believe Oriental tobaccos evolved from the American seed, but the Europeans did introduce tobacco seed to this region about a century after they discovered the New World. Historians know that tobacco was growing in Turkey in 1603, and perhaps earlier. Historical evidence reveals that there was some cultivation of tobacco in Thrace by the middle of the seventeenth century, but the date of the introduction of the first seed is not known. In any event, Oriental tobaccos are dramatic examples of the adaptation of the plant to different soil and climate.

Major names of Oriental tobaccos, such as Xanthi and Samsun, generally represent districts, not unlike the nomenclature of French wines. Oriental tobaccos vary in flavor, color, and aroma from district to district, as do the tobaccos of the flue-cured growing belts of the United States.

There are two basic classifications: Orientals and semi-Orientals. While the semi-Orientals possess similarities to the Oriental tobaccos in taste, they are heavier in body

Imaginary figures, engraved in 1735, are clothed from head to foot in tobacco. They carry flowering plants, tobacco rolls, and implements used in processing the leaf. Behind them, men operate a press (r.) and a roller.

and not so fragrant. Semi-Orientals are grown in areas bordering Oriental growing regions. They are not very important in world trade.

Most authorities consider true Orientals to be produced in Thrace and Macedonia, which are now in the northeastern portion of Greece; peninsular Greece; southern Bulgaria and Yugoslavia; some of the Aegean islands; the western end of Turkey, centured around Izmir; northern Turkey, bordering the Black Sea; Anatolia, the northeastern portion of Turkey across the Bósporus; the southern portion of Russia, around the north shore of the Black Sea, principally in the Crimea; and Cyprus.

Western Europeans began to develop a taste for this type of tobacco after the return of British and French soldiers from the Crimean War (1854-1856), where they had fought alongside the Turks against Russia and developed a taste for Turkish cigarettes. (Cigarettes still account for the major consumption of tobacco throughout the Middle East.) The importation of Oriental tobaccos into Western Europe and America increased from that time on, not only to be used in cigarettes but also because of the demand by pipe smokers, the English in particular, to have these tobaccos mixed with Virginias.

For years manufacturers have been using names of Oriental tobaccos to increase the mystique of their mixtures. Many of these names, however, do not describe the Oriental tobaccos actually used in the mixtures.

The most important regions that supply English and American manufacturers are Thrace, Macedonia, north-central Turkey, extreme western Turkey, and Cyprus. Each area's produce has its distinguishing marks.

Western Turkey—Here the famous Smyrna tobacco is grown in the vicinity of Izmir. It is the most aromatic and full-bodied Oriental tobacco, but it is rather dark in color and has a tendency to burn poorly.

Cyprus—This island also grows the Smyrna type. The Cypriots either sell the tobacco in the standard yellow Oriental form or they fumigate it to make Latakia.

North-Central Turkey—Samsun-Bafra tobacco is grown in the vicinity of these two cities—a very delicate, lightly colored tobacco, and the most light-bodied of all Orientals.

Thrace—Around the city of Xanthi is grown the very famous Xanthian leaf, deemed by some to be the finest Oriental tobacco. It is very light-bodied. The area also produces Yenidje, a somewhat more full-bodied tobacco.

Macedonia—The tobacco-growing industry centers around the cities of Kaválla, Drama, Salonika, and Katerini, and grows a medium-bodied type.

Oriental tobaccos are identified by the topographical areas in which they are grown. Yaka refers to those tobaccos grown on the upper slopes of low mountain ranges,

Deep water along Chesapeake shoreline permitted ocean-going ships to anchor at plantation landings (top) and on-load hogsheads of tobacco for Old World (c. 1660). Bottom: Barrels are rolled to market along "tobacco road" in 1830.

Krul Tabak

UIT DE

STOOM TABAKSFABRIEK

van

CORNELIUS ONNES

STEENTILSTRAAT.   GRONINGEN

BAAI-TABAK.

Stoom-Tabaksfabriek.

Deze en meer andere soorten van Marij-
land, Portorico, Varinas, Shag en Pruimtabak
zijn te bekomen bij H. W. HECKMAN IJ.zn,
Nieuwe Ebbingestraat lett. N, No. 47.
te Groningen.

2½ H.G.

Djebel to those grown in the mountains, and Ova to those grown in plains areas or on lower lands in richer soil. Djebel tobacco plants have very small leaves of excellent quality. The Yaka leaf is very delicate, has few stems, and is of high quality. Ova tobaccos are larger plants with a lower-quality leaf.

Oriental tobacco seeds are sown as early as January in the Balkan areas; for most other areas, sowing begins in March. After about three months, good seedlings are taken to prepared fields and spaced rather closely; proximity creates a small plant with tender

leaves. Little is done to the plants until harvesting. Within five weeks to two months after planting, the lower leaves begin to ripen. Just before full ripeness, when the leaf is a yellow-green, the field workers begin priming it.

Leaves brought from the field are strung on a cord run through the midrib of each leaf. The strings of tobacco are set in the shade for a few days, until they have wilted and almost completely yellowed in color. Next they are hung in the sun until completely dry. This can take from a week to a month depending on the type of leaf—the finer, more fra-

164

BAAI TABAK № 2

DE TABAKSPLANT

Deze en meer andere soorten van Tabak Sigaren Thee, Koffijboonen, Specerijen, Kruideniersswaren enz. zijn te bekomen bij

P. H. PFEIFFER.
Poelestraat 36
te GRONINGEN.

De Tabakshandel

Deze en meer andere soorten van Tabak. Koffie, Thee, benevens alle soorten van Kruideniers- waren, Verfstoffen, Specerijen en Sterke dranken zijn te bekomen bij

J. SWAAGMAN I.zn.,
ten Oosten in de Nieuwe Ebbingestraat,
Lett. O, No. 28, te *Groningen*.
2½ H.G.

grant top leaves generally take the longest to dry. Drying in the sun helps to set the color of the leaf. After drying, the leaf is allowed to absorb moisture from the air to become more pliable, and then is packed into bales.

There are no auctions in the Oriental districts. A year's crop is sold in farm lots directly to buyers who process and ferment the tobacco. These dealers, or brokers, in turn sell the tobacco to merchants all over the world.

Oriental leaf grown in countries out- side the principal growing regions seldom reaches world trade. It is used mainly in the countries in which it is grown for the manu- facture of cigarettes. Oriental tobaccos amount to about eight percent of the world crop.

Latakia and Perique, along with light Oriental types, are grouped as condiment, or flavoring, tobaccos. Latakia probably has the richest and most pungent aroma of all natural tobaccos used in blending. Latakia gets its name from the Syrian port of Al Ladhiqi- yah. No one knows who started producing Latakia but perhaps some Syrian farmer, hav- ing an amount of unsold Oriental tobacco at the end of a season, hung the leaf in his home

Dutch tobacco trademarks in extensive
collection of Theodorus Niemayer,
a distinguished old company established
in 1819. Beehive and "De Tabakshandel" (The
Tobacco Trade) were marketed
by Niemayer in 1874 and 1887, respectively.

L. Boilly

DELICIOUS WEATHER.

London Publish'd February 13th 1808 by H. Humphrey 27 S.t James's Street

Etch'd by J. Gillray

A Cure for Drowsiness — or —

A PINCH of CEPHALIC

where it was cured throughout the winter by smoke from the wood he burned for warmth. Resins from the smoke would have seeped into the leaf, making the tobacco more pungent.

Latakia used to be processed from a Syrian type of Oriental known as Shek el-Bent, a tobacco with a comparatively high nicotine content. It was stalk-cured—cut, wilted, and cured in the sun. Still on the stalk, it was then hung in tightly sealed sheds and fumigated with smoke of local species of oak and pine. The various woods were burned in rotation, two weeks per type, for about two months. After the fumigation was completed, the leaves were stripped from the stalks, pressed into bales, and allowed to ferment.

Syria no longer produces Latakia. Production was suspended because the supplies of native wood were being depleted. Today it comes from Cyprus, where Oriental tobaccos of the Smyrna type are grown. The Cypriots sell the tobacco both in standard yellow Oriental form and fumigated (processed as above) for Latakia. The higher grades are very fine Latakia tobacco.

Perique is unique to the St. James Parish of Louisiana. In the 1750s, a French colonist, Pierre Chemot, observed Choctaw and Chickasaw Indians of Louisiana pressing local tobaccos in hollowed-out logs. The pressure caused the tobaccos to release their natural juices and the Indians allowed the leaf to steep in this juice. Chemot perfected this type

Left: Daumier and Boilly lampooned French snuff-takers (top), while James Gillray spoofed England's sneezing squires (bottom). Right: Thomas Gainsborough's imposing portrait of "John Scrimgoeur" fixes a moment of 18th-century time.

167

of processing and developed the fragrant tobacco to which he gave his nickname, Perique.

Today only about twenty growers produce on the average 150,000 pounds of this leaf a year. The seedlings, sown in December and January, are transplanted in March to the fields. Perique is then handled much like Burley, except that each Perique plant is topped to mature only eight to ten leaves. In July, the ripe plants are stalk-harvested and hung in a curing shed for about fourteen days until uniformly brown. The tobacco is stemmed and stripped from the stalk, put into one-pound bundles, and placed in oak barrels and pressed. After two weeks under heavy pressure, the tobacco is removed, aired, and cooled, then repacked and repressed. This procedure is repeated twice. Manufacturers continue processing it for about ten months. The pressure causes the tobacco to turn brownish black or black. About eighteen months after planting, Perique is ready to be aged.

In the 1800s and early 1900s, Perique was used to a large extent in chewing tobaccos, cigarettes, and some smoking mixtures. However, its major role will always be in high-grade mixtures for the pipe. It is indispensable in making fine English mixtures, adding spice and aroma without adding bite. It is too heady to be smoked by itself.

The Manufacturing Process

Before reaching the consumer all tobaccos are subjected to procedures which enhance their flavors and give them distinct burning characteristics. The manufacturing process can transform leaf into a wonderful smoking product or reduce it to an unpalatable one.

The first step in the manufacturing process is the softening of aged leaf in a thermal vacuum machine where enough moisture is added to the tobacco to make it "workable," so that it will not break when handled. Tobaccos to be used in blends in their natural state are then passed through a conditioning cylinder. More moisture is added at this stage to make the tobacco ready for cutting—tobacco must be limp when it is cut to keep breakage to a minimum.

The various tobaccos used in a flavored, or cased, blend are thoroughly mixed together in a revolving conditioning cylinder. The next step is casing. The tobacco is submerged in a tank containing the flavoring mixture or sprayed with it. The tobaccos are then put through a drying machine. If the cased tobacco is not to be pressed into cakes or plugs, it is loosely packed in wooden boxes or barrels and stored until the flavoring is completely absorbed.

If the cased tobacco is to be made into cakes and plugs, it is formed into tightly compressed square or rectangular masses in a hydraulic forming press. The average size of the plugs is about sixteen square inches, three-quarters of an inch to three inches thick.

What is probably the oldest-known tobacco wrapper appears on pewter plate in 1644 painting by Dutch artist Hubert van Ravesteijn. In foreground is a bundle of spills, wooden splinters which were lit by candle or fire and used to ignite tobacco.

168

Orien-
tael   Verginis
               Toback

Tot Dordrecht
Inde nieustraet in blienbergh - A° 1644

Cutting is an important step because, in addition to giving different blends a distinct appearance, it enables the master blender to create nuances of flavor in mixtures. Also the smoker will find certain cuts stay lit better than others, depending on his smoking habits.

Conditioned natural and cased leaf which has not been pressed into cakes or plugs is cut in the following basic forms:

Fine cut—Very narrow ribbons of tobacco, often as fine as that used in cigarettes.

Ribbon cut—Strands one to two millimeters in width. This is the standard cut for high-grade English mixtures.

Square cut or double cut—Square flakes of tobacco roughly three to five millimeters square. This tobacco is cut into a broad ribbon and then turned and cut again.

Granulated—Small, irregular pieces of tobacco generally no more than four millimeters across at any point. This unattractive cut is made by pounding it through a steel mesh screen which cuts it apart.

Rough cut—Partially broken "slices" of unpressed cased Burley. This is similar to a ribbon cut, except the strands of tobacco adhere to one another creating "slices."

Ready rub, crushed plug, or cut plug—Double-cut chunks approximately two by four millimeters made from cased Burley or Cavendish.

Cake and plug tobaccos may be cut as follows:

"A Tobacco Merchant with His Two Sons" (above)
examines a shipment of tobacco on the bank
of a canal in 18th-century painting
by P. S. Henrich. Left: Bas-reliefs on
undated wooden plaque show smokers and group
(center) making twists and plugs.

*Pair of 18th-century paintings by the
Belgian artist Léonard Defrance
show visiting burghers complacently watching
children at work sorting tobacco leaves
and coiling "rope." Huge shipping casks are two
to three times the size of colonial hogsheads.*

Flake (English) or sliced plug (American)—Small rectangular cakes that have been sliced and then left in cake form, much like loaves of bread. This tobacco is generally cut in slices about a millimeter in thickness.

Sliced cake, cut cake (English), or sliced broken plug (American)—Cakes cut in the same manner as sliced plug and flake, but then rubbed out to a degree before packaging.

Cube cut—Double-cut plugs or cakes that are dense little cubes of tobacco from two to five millimeters in size.

Sliced roll and spun cut—Circular slices of tobacco up to one-and-a-half inches in diameter, no more than one-and-a-half millimeters in thickness.

Sliced plug (flake) tobaccos are weighed and packaged for shipment at this point. The ready-rub and rough-cut tobaccos, if they are not to be used in mixtures, are sprayed with a distinctive "top dressing" of flavoring before being packed for shipment. The cut-cake and sliced broken-plug tobaccos, if they are not to be mixed with other varieties, are also packaged after cutting.

A mixture contains various cuts of different tobaccos in specified quantities. By simply varying cuts within a single mixture and thus controlling the rates at which they will burn, the manufacturer can alter the flavor of his product to some degree. (Of course, the proportion and types of tobaccos used, as well as the flavorings, will affect the

174

Cigar-end scraps wrapped in paper originally
were a poor man's smoke until the fashion for cigarettes
caught on, about 1800. Thereafter they were big
business, particularly in Seville, where
Spanish Carmens, like those in Constantin
Meunier's painting, rolled them by hand.

final taste more than the cut.) Mixtures are matured before being packaged for shipment. Some mixtures require pressure and aging to reach peak smoking condition (for instance, some English mixtures); others are simply stored in containers to mature.

The manufacturing process requires artistic as well as scientific skill. The master blender's creativity and sensitivity of palate are perhaps the most important factors in the production of fine smoking tobaccos.

Manufactured Tobaccos

The maze of different blends, mixtures, and straight tobaccos in tobacco shops today can be confusing even to experienced pipe smokers. With wine, for example, one can always be sure he is buying a Burgundy or a Bordeaux because of the strictly regulated classifications. The same is true of cheese and spirits—products that cater to man's sense of taste. This, however, is not always the case with tobaccos. The smoker, after trying one particular blend that is not quite to his liking, may buy another with a different name, assuming it will be a completely different type of tobacco. This may not be the case, however, because of confusing and contradictory nomenclature.

Naturally, a professional tobacconist has a thorough knowledge of the products available and, after exploring the smoker's likes and dislikes in tobaccos, will probably be able to find a mixture or a group of two or three mixtures or straight tobaccos that will satisfy his customer. Unfortunately, though, this sort of tobacconist is a member of a rather rare breed; in most cases it is left to the customer to plod along by trial and error, spending a great deal of money for very little satisfaction. Matters are further complicated by the fact that terms to describe the qualities of tobacco are loosely used within the industry. It is difficult in most instances to ascertain exactly what is in a can by reading the label.

Let me define the terms which will be used here to describe pipe tobaccos.

Aroma refers to the fragrance of the tobacco, in the can and as it is being smoked. Unless the smoker has considerable experience with all types of tobacco and is able to judge what type of leaf has been used, the aroma when the can is opened is, in most cases, no more than a gentle advertisement which sometimes proves to be false. A smoker cannot adequately judge the aroma of a tobacco as he smokes—it can only be measured by the comments he receives.

Flavor refers to the basic taste of the tobacco. This can be measured in three ways: First, the type or nature of the flavor, such as "fruity," "nutlike," "spicy," "natural," or "Oriental." Second, the intensity of flavor or richness can be measured by using the terms "mild" (which refers to tobacco that is light in flavor), "medium," and "full" (referring to a tobacco with a great deal of flavor). Third, the

A variety of packaged tobaccos for pipes and, in drawstring sacks, for cigarettes. Names and labels proliferated, but "Bull Durham," which first appeared in 1865, reigned as world's most popular brand for more than fifty years.

177

flavor of tobacco can be analyzed with regard to its sweetness. "Naturally sweet" refers to a tobacco with the rather subtle sweetness one gets from some natural leaf to which flavoring has not been added. Then there are "lightly sweet," "sweet," and "very sweet." These graduated measurements apply to flavored or aromatic tobaccos.

Body refers to the feeling one gets from the tobacco as it is smoked. The fact that a tobacco has an intense flavor does not necessarily mean it will be full-bodied. For example, very mild, lightly flavored Burley tobaccos tend to be more full-bodied—that is, have a more aggressive effect on the palate— than some full-flavored types of leaf. Body, then, is directly related to the strength or depth of the character of tobacco rather than to its taste.

Light-bodied tobaccos are gentle; medium-bodied are robust but not strong; full-bodied are hearty. "Strong" tobaccos can be classified as "gutsy"; there is no delicacy in tobaccos labelled "strong."

Smoothness is the result of a fine balance between the flavor and the body of a tobacco. When a mixture tastes good, is not overpowering, and is not harsh in any way, it is smooth. Smoothness is so subject to individual taste it cannot be classified by degrees.

Smoothness is greatly dependent on processing. Smokers often shy away from one blend or another because it contains a mixture of tobaccos similar to brands they have tried without satisfaction. Because one manufacturer's mixture was not smooth, they are afraid to try others of the same type. This is faulty reasoning—another brand may prove to be very satisfying.

I have devised a classification system for tobaccos on the American and European markets. Each group is explained as precisely as possible as to basic components and the range of quality products available. The five classifications of tobacco—American, English-Scottish, Irish, Dutch, and Danish—are named for countries. Over the years each nation cited has produced its own distinctive tobaccos for pipe smokers. Recently, however, because of the expanding market, various countries have begun to produce a wider range of types, so that they now overlap one another. We find, for example, Dutch and Danish companies now producing tobaccos for the American aromatic taste and some American companies producing high-grade English tobacco.

There are just two basic types of manufactured smoking tobaccos that are truly American: the straight Burley plug and the "American" mixture, which is a cut form of the Burley plug mixed with a flake-cut Virginia tobacco. "American" is the designation for those tobaccos which evolved in the United States, with respect not only to the way they are grown and cured, but also to the methods by which they are produced.

With the founding of the new nation, Americans were eager not only to grow but also to process the tobaccos they had so long exported to England and Europe for processing. As American manufacturers became more numerous, more "American" manufactured tobaccos began to appear. In the beginning these products were fashioned for the most part after English brands with which the Americans were familiar.

There was not a great variety, nor was the tobacco of high quality. A few varieties of compressed or twisted tobaccos, all of a straight type, led in popularity then and were used both for chewing and smoking. Some early mixtures were manufactured as well. At the time of the Civil War there was a shift in emphasis from the dark Virginia types to the Burleys of the inner states. The new bright Virginia leaf gained in popularity after the war, but the bulk of this leaf was used by the cigarette industry or exported. This is true today. Now the twists and strong plugs have vanished from the pipe smoker's vocabulary and the industry is producing lighter cakes and plugs almost entirely from modern Burley, or using it combined with some flue-cured leaf as the basis of mixtures.

Straight American tobaccos are any of the straight White Burleys available, no matter what other names they may be given, such as Kentucky Burley and Tennessee Burley. These types are offered in a fairly wide variety of cuts. The most popular of these is the cut or crushed plug. They are also found in cube-cut form, which varies in coarseness among manufacturers. Another type, though it is not as popular today as it was years ago, is the sliced plug.

All of these straight Burleys are flavored, to a greater or lesser degree, by the manufacturer. Except for the initial aroma, straight Burleys are pretty much the same, although their smoothness varies considerably depending on the grade of leaf used and how it is processed.

Burley is a straightforward tobacco. While it has a bland taste that is mild in character, it generally possesses a rather full body. When well-seasoned and aged, Burley can provide a mellow smoke. If not carefully processed and aged, it tends to be flavorless and, instead of being smooth, becomes overly robust, even harsh. Burley is exceptionally slow-burning. Naturally, the broad or coarse versions are the slowest burning, but all types, if properly handled, make an acceptable smoke in or out of doors. There are other naturally flavored straight tobaccos that are smoother than straight Burley, but it is good for those who prefer a very mildly flavored tobacco with noticeable body. It is especially good as an all-day smoke.

The word "aromatic," applied as it often is to those tobacco mixtures that have been flavored in varying degrees, is a mis-

nomer. "Aromatic" really is a name given to Oriental tobaccos. It would be less confusing if the smoker referred to these mixtures as "flavored" or, better, "fragrant" mixtures. This type of mixture generally is based on some form of cut-plug Burley tobacco mixed with varying grades of flake-cut Virginias plus, occasionally, some Turkish, Latakia, Cavendish, or Black Cavendish tobacco. It is the product most generally associated with American production.

Unfortunately, most of the fragrant mixtures offered on the American market are mediocre. The exceptions are some of the higher-priced varieties which are made from excellent leaf and are expertly processed. The problem with most fragrant mixtures is that they involve a basic blend of tobaccos that cannot stand on their own. Any high-quality mixture depends on the use of high-grade leaf. If a blend is poorly conceived prior to processing, inferior characteristics cannot be completely muted by even the finest processing techniques or by flavoring compounds—which

The Inspector of Tobacco

A WAREHOUSE.

TOBACCO WAGONS | THE SALE | BIRTHPLACE OF "LONE JACK" TOBACCO

run the gamut from plums to coconuts.

The flavorings applied to fragrant mixtures are so diverse that it would be useless to try to catalogue all of them. Conversely, however, there is a rather narrow range of basic tastes to be experienced within this group. Almost all of them when smoked produce a mild to medium intensity of flavor, generally not distinguishable from the initial aroma of the tobacco in the can. The basic taste characteristic is that non-rich flavor derived from Burley and Virginia, which may be as much

as ninety percent of the blend.

Body is dependent on the grade of leaf used and how it was seasoned, if at all. These mixtures run from light through full in body, the mixture being lighter in proportion to the amount of Virginia used. Burning characteristics vary greatly, from the rather fast-burning, finer-cut types to the medium to slow-burning varieties that contain a great deal of coarse, cube-cut Burley or rubbed, broadly sliced plug.

The smoker who prefers these types

Above: Sketches of tobacco world
of Lynchburg, Virginia, in early 1900s.
Left: Stalks of harvested Burley
are spiked onto laths taken
from bundle on frame in rear
preparatory to the curing process.

181

should analyze all their smoking characteristics by sampling and comparing mixtures that interest him. The fragrant mixture has a way of being more deceptive than other types. Almost all the standard, inexpensive brands fail to produce a flavor that coincides with the initial aroma or the fragrance released in the room as they are smoked. Also they generally do not provide the smoothness one should expect from a quality tobacco. The fragrant mixture when well produced, regardless of the flavors used for aroma, should be a pleasant, light- to medium-bodied blend that endures as a good, all-day smoke.

Almost all tobaccos produced in America contain flavoring to a greater or lesser degree. The typical tobacco in this group is a mixture that depends almost totally on the addition of artificial or natural flavorings for its distinctive taste or aroma. The occasional use of Latakia or Perique tobaccos in small amounts has virtually no effect on the basic taste of these blends. In a fine, fragrant tobacco, on the other hand, there is a relationship between the initial aroma and the taste the smoker experiences while smoking. Fragrant mixtures are not always produced from cut-plug and flake tobaccos. Ribbon-cut, non-plug Burley and ribbon-cut Virginia tobaccos are used occasionally. Nevertheless, we are dealing here with the same light-bodied base.

American-Oriental tobaccos include two types of mixtures. One has a Burley base containing large percentages of Virginia, light Orientals, dark Orientals, and American condiment tobaccos. These mixtures are not flavored and are intended to give the smoker Oriental taste characteristics. They are lightened considerably in intensity, however, by the Burley base. Generally, American-Oriental mixtures of this type appear in the traditional cut-plug and flake form. Occasionally they are found in a ribbon cut. These mixtures usually are preferred by individuals who enjoy the character and smoothness of Oriental tobaccos but find them too rich. Unfortunately, they seldom are produced from quality leaf.

The second type of mixture classified American-Oriental differs from the first in that it is flavored. These mixtures are produced in the same cuts as the first group. Manufacturers of such mixtures frequently use the flavorings merely as cover-ups for low-grade tobaccos and poor seasoning procedures.

American-Oriental mixtures in almost all cases have distinct Oriental overtones. Their flavor ranges from mild to full. Sometimes the flavor is close to that of English-Scottish mixtures. However, the Burley base gives these mixtures more body. Excellent American-Oriental tobaccos may pleasantly surprise the smoker, but when these mixtures are poorly executed, they lack balanced flavor characteristics and have a tendency to overpower the smoker because they lack smoothness.

Earlier Times: Hogsheads of Burley with hulls removed (top l.) are displayed for inspection by prospective buyers. Top r.: Bundles of fresh-cured Burley ready for auction. Bottom: Factory workers stem and process tobacco by hand.

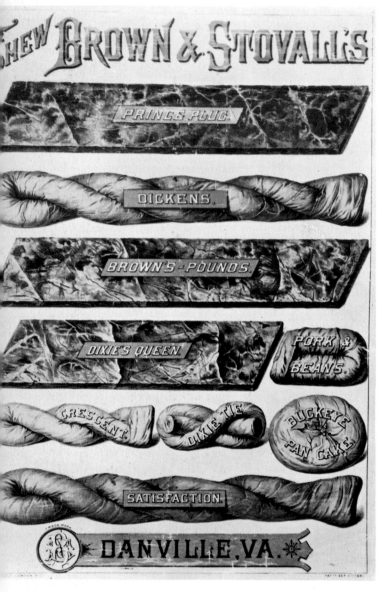

Within the group of English-Scottish tobaccos lie virtually all the mixtures and straight tobaccos that have been held in the highest esteem by connoisseurs for decades. In the early days of manufacturing, tobaccos of both England and the United States were harsh, dark, and heavy-bodied. With the production of flue-cured, bright Virginia tobaccos, however, processing of tobacco in England and the United States began to differ.

In the United States, between the Civil War and the turn of the century, Burley became the standard tobacco for the pipe smoker. In England, on the other hand, the bright, new, Virginia tobaccos proved to be the ideal base for the Oriental and condiment tobaccos the English had enjoyed for years. The new Virginia also proved to be popular in English cakes and rolls, and because of its delicate flavor it soon replaced the darker varieties.

Today, as at the turn of the century, English and Scottish tobaccos are preferred by connoisseurs in virtually every country. Although they no longer are manufactured solely within the British Isles, the greatest quantities are still produced there.

English-Scottish straight tobaccos, which are also classified as "Matured Virginias," are made with very few exceptions from high-grade Virginia. Nearly all these straight Virginias are manufactured in a compressed form, after which they are cut in ways which more or less correspond with the cuts of

One of the last wooden Indians in Brooklyn (r.) stood his ground until 1930. "Chaw" also was diminishing by then. Brown & Stovall's poster from the heyday of chewing tobacco, advertises an array of flat plugs and twists bearing exotic brand names.

American straight Burleys.

A Matured Virginia starts with a blend of varying types of flue-cured tobaccos in strip form. Instead of flavoring the leaf, its moisture content is increased to a point that allows a natural interaction between the leaves during an extended period of seasoning or maturing. Heat is used to hasten this interaction.

The excellence of Matured Virginias is dependent upon the basic richness and other fine properties of choice leaf. Virginia contains the highest quantity of natural sugar of any tobacco. Before maturation it has a tendency to be overly piquant or zesty, but it gains mellowness and loses its edge after it has matured. It takes a great deal of talent to judge and control the seasoning of Virginias.

One can find a variety of subtle differences in flavor among the many versions available. Some products that appear rich and have a fine aroma in the can may have matured too long. Others are too moist. The result in both instances is a smoke that lacks character in its flavor and body, and in the latter a thin, wet vapor is produced that is extremely annoying. In recent years some companies have begun to use Virginian leaf grown in India or southern Africa. These tobaccos, except those from Rhodesia, are cheaper than those grown in the United States and they do not possess the excellence of flavor and basic character of American Virginia tobaccos.

HALF NAKED LOVING NATURAL AND GREEK.

A fine Matured Virginia is somewhat analogous to an excellent Cognac. It possesses an alluring initial aroma that is neither light nor heavy and, although it is not so penetrating as the aroma of Cognac, it is similar in that both products remind one of a subtle mixture of rare fruit and spices in which no single ingredient overpowers another.

The taste of straight Virginias is not as rich as the flavor of Oriental tobaccos, but it is rich enough to satisfy the smoker and it never tires him. Fine straight Virginias are smooth, but they would never be classified as soft or delicate because, while they possess a rather light taste and are never stronger than medium in body, their character is zesty and tangy. This is a tobacco that never goes flat. And rather than getting harsher as one smokes close to the bottom of the bowl, it improves. Matured Virginias are tobaccos that suit almost any type of smoker. They provide a good all-day smoke for the man who cannot smoke tobaccos that are richer or heavier in body. Furthermore, they are well-suited for morning smoking for those who prefer something lighter than usual at that time of day. The broader-cut varieties are superb for smoking outdoors or while active.

Matured Virginias are offered in a number of different forms. The sliced, unrubbed cake or flake is a very compact form that gives the smoker the option of rubbing

Commercial magic of Durham's Bull prodded competitors to artistic excess in turn-of-the-century posters and labels. Don Juan implied passion, Blue Grass spouted cheerful doggerel, Lorillard and Daniel Scotten still invoked the nearly decimated noble savage.

out the tobacco to any consistency he desires. This probably is the most popular form. Cake that has been rubbed out by the manufacturer is also available from finely cut varieties, which are suitable for those who smoke slowly, to coarse versions that are ideal for the vigorous smoker. Yet another form is the sliced roll or sliced bar. The sliced roll usually consists of nothing more than Virginias that have been spun into a long roll of the same density as the cake, sliced rather thinly, and arranged in a tin to serve the same purpose as flake tobacco. Bar tobaccos are produced in a similar manner.

The manufacturers of rolls frequently stray from using only Virginia tobaccos in their products to spin in some Perique, a perfect complement. The result is a product with a pungent aroma and a fuller body than straight Virginia. The taste of the Perique is not distinguishable in itself, but the total taste is a little more intense because of its presence. Matured Virginias usually are somewhat more expensive than other straight tobaccos; most smokers consider them worth the price.

English-Scottish blends probably are the most noble of all mixtures made for the pipe. No flavoring agents or heavy casings are used in their manufacture. Their aroma, flavor, and softness are derived from the use of the choicest leaf blended and seasoned skillfully by craftsmen. The knowledgeable smoker generally favors these fine tobaccos. When choice, unflavored Virginias, Orientals, and dark condiment tobaccos are blended and matured, the result is a product that offers distinct flavor characteristics, smoothness, and an exceptionally light body. Production of English-Scottish blends is similar to that of other mixtures, except that more work is done by hand and, of course, no casings or flavorings are added. The production of English-Scottish blends, as with Matured Virginias, involves a rather lengthy seasoning process to insure a complete "wedding" of the various types of leaf used, and also to eliminate the slight edge of the Virginias and light Orientals. However, heavy pressure is not applied to the English-Scottish mixture as it is in the production of Matured Virginias.

Through blending, subtle differences in flavor and intensity of flavor are produced from various mixtures of the natural leaf. Smyrna, Samsun, Xanthi, Katerini, Old Belt, and Middle Belt tobaccos are important in English-Scottish mixtures. Old Belt Virginia (Piedmont Virginia, Red Mottled Virginia, and Red Virginia) is used as a base because it provides richness and substantially more body than lighter Virginia types. Middle Belt Virginia and tobaccos from the other flue-cured belts that are not so full as Old Belt Virginia are used as a base for the lighter-bodied, generally milder mixtures. These tobaccos are also used with the rich Red Virginia tobacco to lighten its body and its intense flavor.

Tobaccos from the Xanthi, Samsun, and Katerini areas are used generously in mixtures that require extremely soft or delicate Orientals, both in flavor and body. Smyrna is used when an exceptionally intense Oriental flavor is desired. It is seldom employed in great quantities, however, because of its poor burning characteristics.

Perique and Latakia are the principal flavoring agents in all English-Scottish mixtures. Without them, a mixture would have little depth. They are important also because their density reduces the rate of burning. In fuller English-Scottish mixtures, Matured Virginia that has been toasted, or stoved, may be used in place of, or in addition to, Perique and Latakia as the dark condiment.

Subtle differences in flavor, intensity, body, and smoothness can be created from the skillful mixing and processing of these tobaccos. English-Scottish mixtures have exceptional character. I would describe their flavor as bordering on a mixture of honey, nuts, delicate spices, and incense. While these tobaccos possess a definite natural sweetness, they would not be classified as "sweet" in the sense that fragrant tobaccos are sweet.

English-Scottish mixtures generally are marketed under the classifications mild, medium, and full. The mild mixture has a light, or mild, flavor intensity and is light in body; it has a tendency, however, to be slightly sharp. The medium mixture is usually well-balanced. It is not so piquant as the mild mixture, having a medium flavor intensity and a slightly fuller body. The full mixture is intense in flavor and aroma owing to the presence of greater quantities of dark condiment tobaccos. Smokers tend to believe a full mixture is the harshest, but the reverse is true. Full English-Scottish mixtures are usually the smoothest.

Of course, the mixtures of one manufacturer will not always correspond to those of another, and indeed most companies produce several mild, medium, and full mixtures. (I produce a mild mixture that appears light in color and aroma, as do most of the milder mixtures, but instead of using a light Middle Belt Virginia for the base I use a light-bodied Macedonian tobacco and a small amount of Virginia. The result is a tobacco that is closer in flavor to a medium mixture that leans toward the mild side. It still is exceptionally light, however, and does not have the usual edge one associates with a mild mixture.)

English-Scottish mixtures are offered in a ribbon cut or, in the case of two or three specific mixtures, in a broad ribbon mixed with a fine cut.

I recommend the English-Scottish tobacco to any smoker, as one can find a variation to suit his taste at any time of day. The most expensive tobaccos are found in this group yet they are well worth the price. These

CIGARS   J<small>NO.</small>FOBLE
1830 - 1926

Mostly the work of unknown craftsmen,
the wooden storefront figure was infinitely
varied. Examples here include
Indian chiefs and squaw, fashionable lady,
Jack Tar, and (holding Mr.
Foble's wares) an unusual Mercury.

GIPSY.

SERVIAN.

HINDOO.

THIBET.

JAPANESE.

CHINESE.

HUNGARIAN.

COSSACK.

KALMUC.

GIPSY GIRL

AMER. INDIAN.

FARMER.

SAILOR.

SIR WALTER RALEIGH.

ENGLISHMAN.

high-quality tobaccos contain no harsh flavorings and are low in moisture content. Two ounces of an English-Scottish mixture generally will go further than two ounces of another type. Also, because of the natural richness of English-Scottish blends, it usually takes fewer bowls to satisfy.

The tobaccos classified as fragrant English-Scottish mixtures and straights are similar to the straight Matured Virginia types and mixtures, except that they have been scented. Almost all scented straight English tobaccos that enter the United States are unrubbed flake tobaccos. These smoke similarly to straight Virginia types but they are a little sweeter and tend to be moist, thus smoking wetter and hotter than the average high-quality straight Virginia.

Irish tobaccos are strongly related to the tobaccos produced in Scotland and England. They are exceptionally sweet and fragrant—a result of the use of intense flavorings. They fall between American "aromatics" and the English scented tobaccos. Irish tobaccos are produced in all the cake forms in which one finds English-Scottish tobaccos.

The Dutch are famous for the production of Cavendish. Even though many Dutch straight tobaccos have been well received on the American market for the past twenty years, the name "Cavendish" continues to be synonymous with the Dutch product. Cavendish tobacco is a mixture of base tobacco leaf, such as Burley and Virginia, that has been flavored in various ways, pressed into a cake, and matured. These tobaccos are usually available in one of two forms: flake, which resembles the English flake or the American sliced plug; and the rubbed-out cake, generally offered in rather long strands similar to the rubbed-out cake Matured Virginias of England and Scotland. This second form is widely known as a Cavendish cut. In addition to being smoked straight, Cavendish tobaccos are used in blends made in other countries, particularly in America and Denmark.

Holland's Cavendish tobacco is exceptionally fine (particularly when one considers the low cost) and is indeed the perfect tobacco for smokers giving up cigarettes, or those who prefer an exceptionally light-bodied, soft tobacco. Flake Cavendish makes an excellent tobacco for the sportsman or anyone who smokes outdoors.

Other tobaccos from Dutch or American-based Dutch companies are diverse. Most of them fall into the category of fragrant mixtures, which more or less resemble many of the typical American flavored products, although they usually are of a higher grade.

Most of the Danish products imported into the United States are copies of types mentioned earlier. The Danish fragrant blends in most cases are subtle and exceptionally high in quality. They rank above the average American type, both in quality of leaf

Cigarette-card series features racial preferences in pipe smoking. Middle Europeans favor wind caps, Asians have small metal bowls and long stems, American Indian has calumet. Englishman appears to be coloring a meerschaum—not too well.

On occasion, wooden cigar-store Indian was neither wooden nor Indian. Puck (far l.) is cast zinc. Others are Goddess of Liberty and Brother Jonathan, precursor of Uncle Sam. Indian princess (r.) has adorned Cambridge, Mass., tobacco shop for nearly a century.

and in processing. Danish Cavendish tobaccos are high in quality also. On the other hand, the tobaccos Denmark produces which suggest (on the can) that they are standard English and Scottish types fall short of the mark. While these Danish mixtures do not come up to a straight Matured Virginia or fine Oriental mixture in quality, they still are of high grade.

These comments about the basic types of tobaccos are general, for the most valuable things to be gained from reading this section are a basic sense of direction in choosing tobaccos and a point from which to begin exploring. I would hope the new pipe smoker, or even the veteran who has not smoked many different tobaccos, would sample at least a few mixtures from each of these classifications in order to be certain he is smoking the tobacco or tobaccos that best suit his palate.

Selecting Tobaccos

Each smoking mixture falls into one of several basic groups, and regardless of slight modifications within each group in types or grades of leaf, cut, or flavorings, each has a basic taste which distinguishes it. If the smoker concentrates on selecting tobaccos from these groups, he will narrow the field and no longer have to wade through a sea of brand names only to find duplications of taste and flavor.

Since enjoyment of a particular tobacco is personal, no one can suggest that one tobacco will be more pleasing than another.

The only guideline is to select high-quality tobaccos, avoiding the lesser copies which abound on the market. Fine tobaccos always smoke cleaner and more smoothly than similar popularly priced brands.

Many smokers feel they should find one perfect blend for themselves. This is not necessarily a good idea. Variety is as desirable in pipe smoking as it is in most areas of daily life. If, rather than buying a large quantity of one tobacco, the smoker keeps smaller quantities of two or three types on hand, he can select one that suits his taste at a particular time. Throughout the day a person's taste changes. In the morning lighter flavors are always more welcome. As the day progresses, richer, more flavorful foods and tobaccos seem in order. I would not eat heavy or spicy foods for breakfast, nor would I smoke a full mixture in the morning. In the evening, though, full mixtures complement a rich meal in a way that lightly flavored tobaccos cannot.

In the warmer months, the smoker may find himself growing tired of certain tobaccos. People eat lighter foods in the summer, and quite often it is more satisfying to change to lighter tobaccos as well.

With the many excellent tobaccos available on the market today, one should find selecting a tobacco not only interesting but quite easy. Once the smoker finds a particular group that he especially enjoys, he should explore it thoroughly, noting the subtle differences among the tobaccos of different manufacturers and among the different blends of one company.

The cut is not critical to a good smoke. It is important only that dense or chunky-cut tobaccos be smoked outdoors because of their slower, cooler burning qualities. Smoking them under windy conditions is safer for the bowl of the pipe and they will taste better. Those who smoke exceptionally hard may also benefit from these cuts. All of the other cuts, perhaps with the exception of the finest, will perform well under any other conditions. The only other consideration is a smoker's preference for one cut or another because it is easier for him to handle.

Far more critical and all too frequently overlooked are smoking habits. If a smoker uses poorly cleaned, oversmoked pipes, he will never get the true taste of the tobaccos. In addition, if he fails to fill and light his pipe properly, the overheated and wet smoke that may be the result will distort the taste. If one is not familiar with how to smoke properly, each smoke is an experiment conducted without controls. The smoker will get a variety of results from the same tobacco and he may by-pass a tobacco that would have been to his liking if he had smoked it correctly.

Storing Tobaccos

Before the development of air-tight rubber seals and the rubber- or plastic-lined pouch, the tobacco jar, the tobacco box, and the pouch were not so functional as they are today. Looking through collections of smoking paraphernalia which date back to the late 1500s, we can see how ineffectual some of them were by today's standards; yet the beauty of the workmanship could not now be equalled. Intricate handcrafted tobacco containers are no longer in vogue. Today's tobacco-related products are functional and plain. No engraved or hand-painted tobacco boxes of gold, silver, and mother-of-pearl, no embroidered linen or beaded pouches are available today.

Smokers of the sixteenth, seventeenth, and eighteenth centuries are glorified in paintings, engravings, and verse. They smoked with refinement, using only the finest handcrafted materials. Some have called it the "Golden Age of Pipe Smoking." Smoking may have been elegant then, but the smoker, despite his bowed shoes and lace cuffs, had to be a hardy fellow, able to withstand and enjoy a smoke which was more rugged than anything we can imagine.

Early paintings and engravings depicting pipe smokers nearly always show long pipes. Until the twentieth century, when the art of pipe manufacturing became a matter of creating a functional inner pipe rather than a highly intricate exterior, the only way smoke could be cooled before reaching the mouth was by passing it through a long stem. The tobaccos smoked during the "Golden Age" were

▲ *Rubbed-out Sliced Burley Plug*　　　　▲ *Cube-cut Burley Plug*　　　　▲ *Dark Sliced Cake (Flake) Virginia*

▲ *Sliced Bar Virginia*　　▼ *Roll (or Spun-Cut) Virginia*　　▲ *Sliced Cord (or Spun-Cut) Virginia*　　▼ *Dark Rubbed-Out Virginia C*

▲ *Rubbed-out Medium-Sliced Virginia Cake*

▲ *Standard-Sliced American Burley Plug*

▲ *Ribbon-Cut Old Belt (Flue-Cured)* ▼ *Double-Cut Perique*

▲ *Square-Cut and* ▼ *Fine-Cut Eastern Belt (Flue-Cured)*

almost always dry because of the way they were processed and the inadequacy of the lovely containers in which they were stored. Not until the twentieth century was it learned that proper moisture content ensures a smoother, more flavorful smoke.

Though most of today's tobaccos are scientifically produced and packaged to ensure the smoker tobacco in the best possible condition, it still is important to store tobacco properly, especially large quantities. The best rule is to buy no more tobacco than can be smoked in three or four weeks, unless it is vacuum-sealed.

The air-tight can in which tobacco is purchased or a tightly sealed tobacco jar is best. Tobacco stored in this manner will not absorb excessive moisture, and will not lose necessary moisture and flavorful oils by evaporation. Many people feel that some sort of moistening device should be put in the jar to keep the tobaccos fresh. If one has a jar or canister that seals well, this is unnecessary.

If the tobacco one buys is dry, it should be returned immediately. A dry mixture cannot be brought back to its original state. By adding moisture to dry tobaccos by means of clay discs, apples, etc., the smoker runs the risk of stripping the tobacco of its natural taste. When the moistened mixture is smoked, the smoker will experience a thin, watery taste. Tobacco jars and pouches are designed to keep tobaccos fresh, not to make

them fresh once they have gone stale.

If tobacco stored in a jar consistently dries out, even with a moisture bottle or similar device, the smoker should buy a better humidor. The industry makes many fine products, but it also has its share of poorly made items. Select a jar with a proper seal. Among those available, products from Denmark, England, Germany, and Japan are superior in most cases to those of American manufacturers.

Flat tins will keep mixtures well if one presses the tobaccos firmly together, places the paper or plastic disc over the top, crimps down the paper jacket surrounding the tobacco, and seals the tin. Tobacco in vacuum-sealed tins with soldered tops that must be cut open should be put in a polyethylene bag and replaced in the can, for once this kind of container has been opened it seals poorly.

Because most European tobaccos come in small two- and four-ounce sizes, it generally is not necessary to worry about them becoming stale; they probably will be smoked before this happens.

From the first days of pipe smoking, man has needed a container in which he could carry tobacco. Today we use the pouch, and I am sure that something resembling it has been used from the beginning. The earliest recorded tobacco containers, however, were tobacco boxes, which were popular from the late sixteenth century through most of the nineteenth century. These containers generally

▲ Burley Strip   ▲ Middle-Belt Strip (Flue-Cured)   ▲ Izmir Leaf

▲ Izmir Leaf ▾ Perique Strip   ▲ Latakia Leaf ▾ Eastern-Belt Strip (Flue-Cured)

were about the size of a small pencil box and came in a variety of shapes—oval, round, even egg-shaped. No niggard with his tobacco, Sir Walter Raleigh kept an unusually large cylindrical one, thirteen inches high, which held at least a pound of tobacco.

During the nineteenth century, the pouch won an increasing number of fans among smokers until it became virtually the only type of tobacco container. Some of the early pouches were made of cloth, but as manufacturers and smokers began to recognize the importance of the moisture content of tobacco less porous substances were sought. Leather fit the need very well.

Today there are two major types of pouches—those which are closed with a zipper and those which fold. (Both can be purchased in leather—the most durable material—with a rubber backing, cloth with a plastic or rubber backing, or entirely of plastic.) Either type will do an adequate job of keeping tobacco fresh but the folded type is superior. The zippered type does have the advantage of opening more easily and most manufacturers make a model of this type that will hold not only tobacco but a pipe, cleaners, and a tool or knife. Any of the quality pouches, no matter what design, perform well if one uses them properly.

When considering a pouch, the smoker should remember that the pouch is meant to supply him for a day and is not meant for prolonged storage. Those who complain of tobaccos drying out in the pouch generally fill it too full, with more than one day's supply. If the smoker does not put leftover tobacco back into a sealed storage container at night, it is possible it may dry out before morning. If one is going to keep tobacco in a pouch for more than a day, the leather, fold-over model is best. With this type the smoker should press the tobacco tightly together and fold the flap around it.

Blending Mixtures

The smoker who is interested in tinkering with tobaccos is faced with an uphill battle. To begin with, any tobacconist or master blender who has succeeded in gaining enough knowledge and competence to produce a wide variety of excellent mixtures will be reluctant to reveal the techniques he uses in creating them. One may find a great deal of free advice from the unskilled, but the professional tobacco blender has spent many years studying the various facets of blending and even if he wanted to explain the art of blending it would be difficult for him to do so without actually showing how it is done. And if the prospective blender could grasp the information the tobacconist might offer, he would be faced with other problems: his inability to find proper tobaccos and his lack of equipment with which to work.

It is difficult to buy the straight matured leaf the professional blender uses. Most of the packaged blending tobaccos are heavily cased and/or flavored. Thus it is difficult for the amateur blender to know what the base and condiment tobaccos taste like naturally. The multitude of names given blending tobaccos is also confusing. "White Burley," "Aged Burley," "Matured Burley," "Tennessee Burley," etc., signify nothing. Burley today *is* White Burley. It is all aged or matured. As for growing location, Burley is pretty much the same from area to area when one compares qualities of the leaf within each given grade.

My only recommendations are that one find a reputable tobacconist and try to obtain the highest grade, near-natural leaf available.

The quality tobacco shop is and always has been both the new and the experienced smoker's key to finding all the products and information he needs to enjoy his smoking. The knowledgeable tobacconist—enriched with an understanding of the subtleties that differentiate the many products on the market —is necessarily a connoisseur who is familiar with all of the fine tobaccos and pipes available. He will never merely push a package of tobacco across the counter in response to a request for "something mild" or "aromatic" or "popular." The uncertain smoker should expect to be questioned concerning his preferences in tobaccos and sometimes foods. The questions may sound trivial, but from the answers he receives the tobacconist generally will have a good idea of what to recommend.

In the seventeenth century, tobaccos were sold by chemists who pulverized and mixed them into compounds for medical use, but as Europeans began to accept tobacco for the pleasure of smoking more and more merchants began to include tobacco in their inventories. From the chemistry shop, tobacco made its way into the grocery. Ale and coffee-houses sold pipes and tobaccos. As smoking proved to be more than a mere fancy, many men abandoned the sale of other items to become tobacconists.

Artisans began to craft finer and more beautiful pipes and accessories, all of which were adopted by eager smokers. By the late nineteenth century, quality tobacco shops were bulging with elegant meerschaum pipes; ivory, amber, silver, and gold pipe tampers and tools; beautiful tobacco boxes and pouches; and jars of pewter, fine china, and rare woods. These shops were more than businesses. They were areas for conversation and enjoyment.

Cigars and cigarettes were the main supports of many of these shops. As far as numbers are concerned, pipe smoking has never been the most popular form of smoking. Yet today we see many cigarette and cigar smokers becoming pipe smokers. It is gratifying to hear their exclamations about the excellent flavors and aromas they had been missing. Today really is the golden age of pipe smoking. The quality of pipes and pipe tobaccos has never been finer.

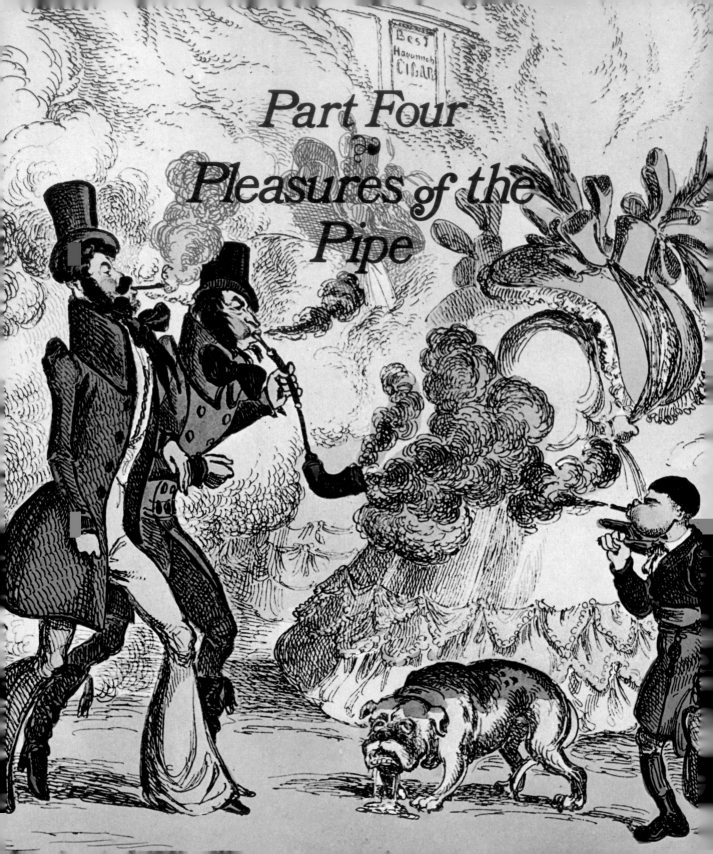

Vell I de sooner have a Pipe of Backer arter a~
but van might as vell be out of the Vorld as ou~
of the Fashio~

A person unaccustomed to any form of tobacco smoking may find pipe smoking much less satisfying than he anticipated. A taste must be developed. As with fine wines, cheeses, and well-prepared foods, one learns slowly to appreciate subtleties of taste and to experience the full enjoyment they can provide. Each form of smoking has its devotees and it is easy to see that it is all a matter of taste.

For me, the pipe is the most enjoyable form of smoking. I know of no other that can stimulate and satisfy as many of the senses as well as it does. The wide range of tobacco types and the many cuts available provide the pipe smoker with an almost endless variety and with the capability of adapting his smoke to different environmental conditions. Briar, gourd, meerschaum, and clay pipes provide increasing visual pleasure as they season slowly, shade by shade, into their simple or intricate patterns, as well as excellent taste.

Merely holding a fine pipe is one of life's pleasures for many smokers.

There is a feeling in today's hurried world that pipe smoking is something of an inconvenience. The fact that there aren't enough knowledgeable sales people to guide smokers properly has contributed to the increasing number of pipe smokers whose expectations go unfulfilled. Pipe smoking is a somewhat more involved pleasure than cigar or cigarette smoking. You must prepare your own smoke and keep your pipes clean. Yet the enjoyment you derive in return makes the effort well worth your while.

The New Pipe Smoker

The initial approach to pipe smoking may be a baffling affair because of the great number of pipes available in varying shapes, finishes, and materials. When a new smoker sees a broad selection of pipes, he may assume that each of them has a completely different set of smoking qualities from the others. This is not

206

true. Inner bowl designs are the same in many pipes which differ in outward appearance. If a smoker is dealing with high-quality, well-designed pipes, almost every one will provide a good smoke.

The new smoker should not spend a lot of money in the beginning. Only the most essential articles—a pipe, tobacco, a tamper, and cleaners—need be purchased. One can then learn how to smoke properly and become accustomed to using these basic items without the confusion that results from having too many "tools." Also, if one finds after an interval that he does not enjoy a pipe for one reason or another, he will not have ventured more than $10 or $12.

I recommend that the new smoker select for his first pipe one of the many fine "seconds" of the better English, French, Danish, Irish, and American pipemakers. As has been mentioned, these pipes do not differ in shape and design from the finest grades, but they contain some fills and sand pits or, in the case of briar, are made of briar in which the grain is not as choice as in the higher price ranges.

The new smoker follows the same basic procedures of filling, lighting, and caring for his pipes as a more accomplished smoker; yet, unaccustomed to the experience, he will have to adjust to the new, perhaps uncomfortable feeling of the bit in his mouth.

The beginning pipe smoker should not concern himself with exploring all types of tobaccos and pipes immediately, because he probably will not notice the subtle differences of flavor and aroma that various tobacco mixtures and pipes produce. Rather, he should concentrate on how a pipe will smoke best for him. Later, when his mouth is not so sensitive and when he can handle the pipe with more assurance, he can try new mixtures and pipes. He then will be able to make a more intelligent selection.

As you gain experience, you will probably settle on a favorite bowl size and

stem design. You will buy pipes because of their appearance, but within that group which you know from experience to be most compatible with your smoking habits and taste. I suggest that you limit yourself at the beginning to medium-sized bowls, as larger bowls will hold more tobacco than your appetite will accommodate. Also they may be too heavy to be comfortable in the mouth.

Thicker-walled pipes will be cooler to the hand and heavier in weight than those with thinner walls. Pipes with bent stems often will put less leverage on the mouth and, even if they are a few ounces heavier than straight pipes, may be more comfortable to hold in the mouth.

I recommend that the new smoker select a rather light-bodied tobacco, such as a Cavendish, light English mixture, straight Burley, Maryland, matured Virginia (English or Scottish), or a high-quality aromatic mixture from a reputable tobacco shop. By beginning with a high-grade tobacco, you will avoid problems you may encounter with the majority of popular blends, which are generally inferior both in the grade of tobaccos used and the degree of attention to detail in cutting and seasoning. The light tobaccos will be less irritating to the new smoker's mouth. Yet, there are those who demand more fullness of flavor from the beginning. Good, full mixtures are not harsh, but their rich flavor has a tendency to wear the new smoker out, affecting him in much the same way too much of a very rich dessert affects a diner.

In the beginning, stay with one tobacco for a week or two, gradually increasing the number of bowls you smoke. Then, when you are accustomed to smoking, branch out and find those types of tobacco that suit your taste best.

A cigarette smoker should consider himself a new smoker and follow these guidelines. He in particular should stay with light tobaccos. Cigarettes are almost always made from light, mild tobacco leaves because they are less harsh to the throat and lungs. When one smokes a cigarette, the pleasure he derives is not one of taste so much as the physical exhilaration of the nicotine from the smoke entering the blood through the lungs. The tongue and soft palate, which are so important in pipe smoking, matter very little to the cigarette smoker. When he begins smoking a pipe, he will react as if he had never tasted smoke. Because he has developed the habit of inhaling, it may be more difficult for him to get used to a pipe. By choosing light tobaccos, the taste and feeling he will experience from pipe smoking will not be terribly unlike that of cigarette smoking. It is not uncommon for newly converted cigarette smokers to inhale pipe smoke; when this happens, richer mixtures are overwhelming.

Perhaps it is best for a cigarette smoker to continue smoking cigarettes while

Adraean Brouwer, 17th-century Flemish master who made smoking a major theme in art, portrayed himself (with tankard) and friends roistering in a country tavern in "The Smokers." Clowning figure (l.) blows smoke through his nose.

209

he begins pipe smoking, gradually increasing the number of bowls he smokes in a day. In this way, he will find cigarettes no longer have the same appeal.

Filling and Lighting the Pipe

One of the most important lessons to learn is how to fill and light the pipe correctly. If the smoker masters these first steps and practices other good smoking habits, all of the rest eventually will fall into place. The smoker will have no problem keeping his pipe lit and will then be free to enjoy the taste of the tobacco, which will improve as the new pipe is smoked.

No one would enjoy smoking a poorly packed cigarette or a poorly rolled cigar, and it seems reasonable to assume the smoker would derive little pleasure from a pipe he had not taken care to fill properly. The same principles pertain to filling cigars, cigarettes, and pipes, with the pipe having the advantage of being adaptable to an individual's taste. To insure a good smoke, one must create an even, close porosity among the strands of tobacco so the pipe will draw almost as firmly as a good cigar before lighting. There are, as far as I am concerned, two methods of filling a pipe: the pinch method and my own.

With the pinch method, one fills the pipe in stages, making sure that each third of the bowl is evenly and firmly packed down, from the draft hole to the top. With my

method, the smoker places enough loose tobacco to fill the bowl in the palm of one hand, filling the pipe by gently but firmly working the tobacco into the bowl with the forefinger of his other hand until the bowl is filled slightly over the top and the tobaccos feel firm when pressed (slightly springy, as a cigarette does). The smoker should make certain the tobacco strands are separated as they are placed in the bowl and that the texture of the tobacco is even and free of clumps which would block a free draft. This method avoids pressure around the draft hole, permitting an easier draw throughout the smoke. In addition, the tobacco will burn to the bottom consistently, with little effort on the part of the smoker. If the bowl has been filled correctly, it should draw firmly, with a little resistance, and the smoker should be able to hear a little air hissing through the pipe.

In the case of very moist tobaccos, fill the pipe more loosely than usual. Otherwise, they may pack down too densely, preventing a good draft and making it necessary to refill the pipe.

While drawing through the stem, light the pipe evenly across the entire surface of the tobacco; then, take your tamper (not your finger) and while you continue to draw, press the expanded tobaccos down evenly all around the bowl until the pipe draws similarly to a cigar—firmly, with no air hissing through. The use of the tamper will dampen the fire to

Figure in Jan Steen painting fills his clay from tobacco cut on a pewter plate before him. This was 17th-century manner of cutting the dried leaves. As demand for pipe tobacco increased, pre-cut tobacco was manufactured for mass market.

a degree, so at this point relight the pipe to get the entire surface of the tobacco burning again. After this second lighting, your tobacco should burn evenly and hence coolly, with little effort. You probably will have to tamp again as the tobacco burns down, since it loosens as it is smoked. Try to maintain the firmness of draw with which you started throughout the smoke. The process is quite easy to master, and with practice will soon become effortless.

When the pipe is packed too loosely, the tobacco burns inconsistently and the smoker has to draw harder to keep it lit, creating more heat. Soon there is nothing but moisture and heat coming through the mouthpiece, and the bowl may burn your hand. At the opposite extreme is the pipe which is packed too firmly. It won't burn at all, no matter what you do—it is as hard to light as a tightly rolled newspaper.

Each tobacco type and cut will smoke slightly differently. The broader, denser types of tobacco are harder to light but they burn more slowly and are particularly good for outdoor smoking because they are not so easily affected by wind as other types are. The reverse is true of the finer cuts, and occasionally they are difficult to handle. Use fine-cut tobaccos with care. They are sometimes recommended for inexperienced smokers because they remain lit no matter how poorly the pipe is filled, but they may blister the tongue.

These two extremes of cut are seldom used alone in preblended tobaccos. They usually are incorporated in blends where their burning qualities complement each other.

When a bowl is filled and lighted properly so that it smokes slowly and evenly, one can derive the intended taste from the tobacco and consider both it and the pipe on their true merits. Many pipes and tobaccos have been mercilessly condemned for causing a variety of problems simply because the smoker failed to understand and master these first steps.

Care of the Pipe

In general, briar, meerschaum, and calabash pipes should be treated the same way. If the smoker regards all of his pipes as delicate, and if he consistently cleans, reams, and rests them, he should always be able to get a good smoke from those that are well suited to his taste and habits.

Smokers who break stems, shanks, and bowls consistently, or who complain about the sour smell of their pipes, obviously are pushing them beyond their capacity to endure punishment. Care in cleaning out the ashes left in the bowl after each smoke with a pipe tool, rather than hammering them out, will be rewarded. There will be a better chance of the bowl remaining unscarred and the frequency with which stems and shanks are broken will be greatly reduced. If the bowl is reamed out

212

Lighting up in 17th-century Flanders is depicted in paintings of David Teniers. In detail (top), a smoker draws a light from a burning coal, while lefthand figure in "The Company of Smokers" uses a "spill" to transfer fire to his pipe. Copper brazier (bottom) is 18th-century Dutch.

frequently, char is prevented from building to a thickness that could reduce the pipe's capacity and increase the danger of its splitting or cracking. It will also prove time-saving in the long run, for each reaming will take just seconds rather than the minutes required for a postponed reaming.

Cleaning and reaming go hand in hand. If the smoker makes a habit of running a pipe cleaner through the stem and shank after every smoke, tars and oils produced during smoking will not have a chance to solidify and clog the draft or affect the taste of the smoke. Pipes that are kept clean never become rank.

The smoker should clean his pipe after every smoke, if possible. Scoop out the ashes with the pipe tool, then run a pipe cleaner through the stem and shank, using both ends of the cleaner. Next, bend the cleaner into a loop that will fit the bowl and swab it out to remove residual particles of tobacco and ash, and also to absorb any remaining moisture.

If a pipe has been allowed to get really dirty, the smoker should use an alcohol-based pipe freshener to break down the tar in the shank. Then he should scour the inside of the channel with a pipe brush and, finally, use enough cleaners to finish the job. Always remember to keep the mortise area at the end of the shank clean, since foul-flavored tars and oils can get trapped there. The bone screw of

214

Antique Accouterments: Ornate Delft tobacco jar of 1707 (top), pair of 19th-century brass tinderboxes (center) with sliding lids and bottoms connected by chain, and tinder-pistol of mid-18th century with flint-and-steel action.

the meerschaum pipe should be kept clean for the same reason. If residue builds up in the area where the stem connects with the shank, pressure could cause the shank to crack, the tenon to shrink (which might create a loose stem), or, in the case of a bone connector, the stem to become misaligned.

Generally, if a smoker uses a preventative maintenance approach to reaming, he will merely have to scrape away the char with the reaming blade of a smoker's knife. If the residue is allowed to build up to over the thickness of a nickel, however, a major job may await the smoker. For the messy pipe, one should buy a heavy-duty reamer—such as the flange reamer—in a fixed size that will fit the bowl. Heavy-duty reamers will seldom cut the carbon to a proper thickness on all the smoker's pipes because they are designed for medium-sized bowls only. The only other reamers on the market that can do an adequate, heavy-duty job are the Savinelli and the Ream-and-Clean adjustable reamers which come with a useful shank reamer.

On heavy jobs one should take special care to center the reamer. Otherwise it will cut the carbon too thin on one side and expose the wall while inadequately reaming the other side. Reaming is as important as any other job in caring for the pipe—and one should do it regularly.

The char that develops within the bowl of a pipe must be controlled, but some is necessary, particularly in the case of briar pipes. A safe thickness of char—that of a dime, or even a nickel for one who smokes very hard —is needed to protect the inner wall from repeated exposure to a burning ember. The best type of char buildup, or cake, consists of an even, firmly grained carbon that will absorb evenly and be durable. To create the ideal kind of cake, fill the pipe properly, using a tamper to pack the tobacco in firmly and evenly.

People who smoke heavily flavored and cased tobaccos will find that they build a soft cake, despite good smoking habits. Sometimes the char is so soft and porous that it can be peeled out with a knife, like the rind of an orange. The smoker who tends to build this type of cake should take the convex spoon end of his pipe tool and, while turning the bowl, press hard against the soft carbon to compress it against the wall of the pipe.

Another type of char that develops is characteristically pitted and uneven. It generally chips away in spots, leaving portions of the bowl unprotected and creating an uneven pressure against the inner wall. This type of char is a direct result of improper filling and smoking. The best remedy is to cut the carbon back until it is even and then begin filling the pipe properly and using a tamper when smoking.

Occasionally the char builds up in the top portion of the bowl and not at the bottom, or vice versa. This results from smoking only part of a full bowl or consistently filling the bowl only halfway. The smoker who develops this sort of cake should buy a few smaller-bowled pipes.

Regardless of how often a pipe is cleaned, it must be well rested to allow the moisture that has been absorbed during smoking to evaporate. Discover for yourself, if you must, the consequences of smoking a pipe constantly: The smoke will lack flavor and taste exceptionally hot and wet. Tobaccos taste much better in a rested pipe.

Pipes should be smoked in rotation and be given a week's rest after each full day of smoking. The owner of a large collection should alternate three or four pipes each day. In this way, no single pipe will be overworked, avoiding a gradual deterioration of taste toward the end of the day.

A pipe should be rested bowl down, in as nearly a vertical position as possible. This allows moisture to run from the shank into the larger space of the bowl, where it will evaporate more quickly. Do not leave a pipe cleaner in the shank and stem of a pipe. The cleaner will, of course, absorb moisture, but if it is left in the pipe the moisture cannot evaporate. Air moving through an open channel will allow the pipe to dry out much faster. When a smoker reams and cleans his pipes properly and allows them to rest, his entire collection will produce the taste that he seeks from his tobaccos.

Not till English genre painters like William Hogarth popularized smoking in art was it held a worthy subject for British artists. One of the first English works to illustrate the habit was Hogarth's "Lord George Graham Smoking in His Cabin" (18th century).

Some Problems and Solutions

The best defense against smoking problems, of course, is the offensive move of learning to smoke properly in the beginning. Providing the smoker develops good habits and is thoughtful about the products he buys, he will have years of smoking enjoyment without being constantly plagued with little irritations.

Nothing would be pleasanter than finding that this section is unnecessary. While the problems are listed individually, they often occur in groups; consequently, the smoker may have to employ several of the remedies in order to solve a compound problem.

Before continuing to specifics, consider the effect of the general physical condition of the smoker upon taste. If one is ill, or taking medication, his pipe will not taste as good as it should. This also holds true when one is excessively tired. Even mints or gum often will alter the smoker's ability to taste accurately. Keep these facts in mind; they often go unnoticed and because of them many smokers have formed impressions of different pipes and tobaccos which are unjust to the products.

Problem: The tongue and mouth are always sore (tingling, burning).

Solution: This generally is a problem confined to the new smoker whose tongue and mouth naturally are quite sensitive. If the soreness persists for more than two or three weeks, it probably can be traced to the fact that the

I hate trouble - tis like physic - only fit for the dogs

smoker hasn't developed good smoking habits. The most common cause of this prolonged irritation is the smoker's failure to fill and light the pipe properly. Other causes might be: smoking too hard and fast, thus creating an excessive amount of heat which burns the tongue and mouth, or smoking a tobacco unsuited to the individual's taste. Filling and lighting a pipe improperly may not only cause an almost unbearable scorching of the tongue, but lead to pipe damage as well, such as splitting or a burned-out bowl.

Problem: The tongue is sore only at the end of the day.

Two stuffy English gentlemen addicted to their long clays are satirized by Henry Heath (l.) and George Woodward (r.), two 19th-century caricaturists of the manners of English gentry.

218

*Happy mortal! he who knows
Pleasure which a pipe bestows;
Curling eddies climb the Room,
Wafting round a mild perfume.*

Solution: Heavy smokers frequently experience this irritation. In order to remedy this situation, consider the possibility of either smoking less or going to a broader-cut tobacco which will last longer in the bowl, naturally smoking cooler. One also might consider switching to a smoother, "natural" tobacco, or perhaps a mixture with fuller flavor which will be more satisfying with fewer bowls than light mixtures tend to be. If none of these suggestions seems to solve the problem, the smoker could be smoking too many bowls in any one of his pipes, not allowing it to rest.

Problem: The pipe tastes flavorless, sour, hot, and wet, and also smells foul.

Solution: Even though the smoker cleans and reams his pipes properly, they will present him with this problem if he does not give them an adequate rest. When the pipe is saturated with moisture and tars, it no longer can perform its task of extracting the various harsh elements from the tobacco by absorbing them. The smoker will complain that his tobacco bites and that the smoke is wet. In addition, if he doesn't clean and ream his pipes properly, they will begin to smell unpleasantly.

Problem: The pipe smokes too wet.

Solution: Besides the reasons given in the preceding paragraph, this problem could also be caused by an extremely damp or heavily flavored tobacco. Or, in poorer quality pipes, it is possible that the draft hole is off-center or too low. If so, particularly in the latter case, one will find more moisture in the smoke. There is no remedy for this problem. All you can do is throw the pipe away.

Another cause which seldom is considered is that in humid climates or during damp periods of the year, any smoke or air that goes through the pipe has a higher moisture content, which condenses in the stem.

Furthermore, if the smoker fills his pipe too loosely and fails to tamp the tobacco after it is lit, he will find he has to draw on the pipe much harder and more often to keep it lit. As he draws, the bowl and smoke become extremely hot, while the channel in the stem is cooled by the drafts passing through it. Condensation of this especially hot smoke in the cool stem chamber will cause a wetter smoke.

Problem: It is hard to keep the pipe lit.

Solution: While the smoker occasionally can blame an exceptionally moist tobacco for this problem, the more common cause is that he has not learned how to fill and light the pipe correctly. On occasion, a smoker will complain that the broader-cut tobaccos are hard or impossible for him to keep lit. He too probably fails to take proper care in filling and lighting his pipes. The smoker should realize also that his pipes should be cleaned regularly, since any blockage of the draft hole or channel by a buildup of tars or tobacco particles will make a free draft impossible.

Problem: The smoke does not seem to last long enough for the capacity of the bowl.

Solution: This again generally is caused by improper filling and lighting. If one does not fill the pipe firmly enough and tamp the tobacco after it is lit, his fill will burn faster and, of course, not last as long as it should.

Another cause of this problem could be exceptionally hard smoking or smoking outdoors in the wind. I suggest that the smoker buy a broader cut of tobacco which will smoke cooler and slower. Also, if the smoker does not ream his bowls and allows the carbon to build up beyond a sixteenth of an inch, he naturally will have a shorter smoke because of the reduced capacity of the bowl.

"Forester at Home," painted in 1866 by the German artist Ludwig Knaus, has woodsman comfortably surrounded by hunting paraphernalia and trophies, while he smokes a traditional porcelain pipe with ornate china bowl, cherry-wood stem, and bone bit.

Problem: The tobacco does not burn evenly across the top. Rather, it tends to burn down the center or down one side of the bowl.

Solution: This is another problem caused by improper filling and lighting. When this occurs, the damage it does, besides wasting tobacco, often goes undetected by the smoker until it is too late. This problem will cause the carbon cake to build up unevenly within the bowl, interfering with a smooth draft by constricting the fill (much the same as pinching a cigar while smoking it would) and causing uneven pressure on the bowl which ultimately could lead to its splitting. The most frequent cause of an uneven burn is a fill which is too loose or unevenly firm. Take care to avoid letting tight clumps of tobacco form when filling the bowl.

Problem: The bowl gets very hot when smoked indoors.

Solution: This is a result of not filling the bowl firmly. The increased heat caused by overdrawing is conducted to the outer surface of the bowl and, whether you are smoking a thin- or thick-walled pipe, the heat will be intense.

One who smokes very hard also may have this problem. The solution is to go to the broader cuts which smoke slower and therefore cooler. The smoker who prefers a finer cut will have to accept the fact that it will always produce a somewhat hotter smoke.

Problem: The bowl gets very hot when smoked outdoors.

Ads for popular smoking tobaccos include "Old Judge," which evidently appealed to cribbage players, and "Bull Durham," a wholesome smoke for the entire family. Right: Nathan Currier (operating without Mr. Ives) idealized bachelor life in "Single" (1845). Far right: Empire smoking stand.

223

Solution: When a smoker is outdoors and active, he probably smokes somewhat harder. This hard smoking, along with a wind or a breeze created by movement, will increase the burning rate of your tobaccos, creating excessive heat both in the pipe and mouth. Even if you are not active, the wind—if it is strong enough—can cause the bowl to overheat. Mixtures containing cube-cut or cut-plug tobaccos, or broad-cut straight tobaccos, or cut cakes (flakes), sliced rolls, and so forth are excellent because they burn slower under these conditions, keeping your pipe and tongue cooler.

Problem: The capacity of the bowl is small because of a very thick cake.

Solution: A smoker should not allow this to happen because pressure on the bowl over a period of time could split or crack the wall. You should not allow more than one-sixteenth of an inch of char evenly covering the inside wall of the bowl. It is better to maintain the cake at this level than to let it build up farther and then having to ream it out.

Problem: The carbon chips away when the bowl is being reamed.

Solution: This is another result of a loosely filled pipe. If the smoker fills his pipe too loosely, he will have to smoke harder and faster to keep it lit. Rather than building up char in the bowl slowly and evenly, a layer of soft and unevenly dense carbon will form. This type of cake provides spotty protection to the inner wall of the bowl and is less ab-

Preceding pages: Memorabilia include a tinder pistol with flint and steel, a shoe snuff box, and a porcelain jockey-head humidor. Left: Posters, tobacco jars, humidors, and tins from yesterday's smoking scene. Right: Lucky Strike ad, c. 1900, promoted Burley pipe tobacco.

227

sorbent than a properly developed, even cake. When this uneven char builds up beyond one-sixteenth of an inch, it has a tendency to flake away when the pipe is being reamed or cleaned, leaving some areas completely unprotected from the heat of the embers. Aside from impairing the ability of a pipe to taste its best, one runs the risk of creating hot spots that eventually could burn out the bowl of a wooden pipe.

Problem: The top of the bowl is scorched.

Solution: It is natural, as you smoke a pipe, for the top of the bowl to darken as oils and tars in the smoke adhere and are absorbed. But scorching of the top of the bowl is caused by carelessness in lighting the pipe, allowing the flame to come in contact with the wood. You can (and should) avoid this by holding the flame away from the tobaccos and drawing it into the pipe. With pipe lighters, do the same or direct the flame straight over the tobaccos rather than at an angle.

Problem: The bowl is cracking or splitting.

Solution: A lack of attention to the buildup of char within the bowl, whether it is uneven or extremely heavy, is the cause of splitting of the bowl in a majority of cases. To avoid this, keep your pipes reamed.

Another reason the bowl may crack is because of inferior and poorly seasoned wood sometimes found in cheap pipes. If the bowl is made of wood that is not completely dry, rapid evaporation of the remaining mois-

Flat lucifers (foreground l.) had a long and sometimes painful history. Potentially explosive, they were not replaced until 1860, when safety match was produced in Sweden. Note variety of containers, and brass match holder (top l.), shaped like hunter's game bag.

ture under the extreme conditions of heat weakens the fiber of the wood and causes the pipe to split.

Problem: The bowl is burning out.

Solution: While reaming a wooden pipe, you may notice an area of the inner bowl wall that is parched and looks somewhat like char. If you probe, you will find that you can dig into the wall easily, sometimes all the way through. This condition inside the bowl generally is accompanied by an extreme darkening of the corresponding area on the outside of the wall. This is known as a burnout.

Though sometimes caused by extremely hard smoking for prolonged periods of time, a burnout in briar generally is caused by "wood burs," a name given to loose ends of wood fiber which have not been removed during manufacture of the pipe. Though burnouts are most frequent in less expensive pipes, they sometimes occur in the finest grades.

When this happens in a fine pipe, the manufacturer will replace it with a new pipe. This is a provision of the warranties, some of which last ninety days, others from a year to a lifetime. If your pipe burns out because of a defect, it will almost always happen within the first month. Some tobacconists are authorized by certain manufacturers to replace your pipe on the spot but, in most cases, the pipe must be sent to the factory for approval.

Problem: The shank has split at the end.

Solution: This is a common occurrence in pipes which are fitted with push-tenon bits. This type of breakage is often caused by the smoker's removing the stem of the pipe when there still is moisture in the shank or when the pipe still is hot after smoking.

When a smoker removes the stem without first cleaning out the moisture, the moisture in the shank runs into the fitted mortise area and swells the wood slightly. Then, when the smoker replaces the stem, the fitting is tighter and, if he proceeds to twist it all the way in, the shank may split. Of course, the danger of this happening is much higher with pipes with thin shanks. A thick shank resists splitting and the tenon may be forced through pressure to shrink slightly, later causing the stem to fit loosely. These problems do not always occur but it is best to clean pipes of this design with the stem in them. Then after allowing them to dry a day or two, it is safe to remove the stem and perform a thorough cleaning.

Problem: An older pipe has been cleaned but the draft is constricted.

Solution: This is usually caused by a buildup of tars in the shank. Use a shank reamer followed by a pipe cleaner that has been soaked in a freshener or alcohol (or a shank brush that has been soaked in a freshener or alcohol) to remove this buildup.

Problem: The shank is broken.

Solution: There is little that can be done about this. Some pipemakers might try to repair the

230

Once merely the subjects of anecdotal painting, smokers became studies in character for late 19th-century Impressionists. This portrait of Père Alexandre, a provincial gardener, by Cézanne is evidence of this subtle shift.

shank by splicing the pieces together or by cutting off the broken end connected to the bowl and refitting it with a new stem. However, competent pipemakers are few and even the best generally will try this only with an expensive pipe. Manufacturers usually guarantee only the bowl.

Problem: Your black (vulcanite) stem discolors (oxidizes).

Solution: This is a common problem. It is usually caused by a reaction of the rubber of the stem to an acidic condition of a smoker's mouth or from prolonged exposure to the sun. The "film" that forms (which has a rather vile taste) generally can be buffed off by a pipemaker by using various grades of abrasive polishes.

When a pipemaker is not available, one could try using a buffer. A smoker would be better off, however, using Savinelli's stem-polishing paste as directed, or scrubbing the moistened bit with baking soda with a fine toothbrush.

Problem: The stem (push-tenon type) fits loosely.

Solution: Although a rubber stem may contract or shrink under certain conditions, this problem is almost always caused by the smoker who insists on pulling the stem out of his pipe when it either is hot or still contains moisture in the channel from an earlier smoke. When he pulls the stem out under either of these conditions, the exposed inner portion of

the shank fitting, or mortise, may swell. If the shank does not crack as he reinserts the stem into this smaller area, the tenon may be forced to shrink by the heat, or the heat and pressure exerted by the swollen wood. When the wood dries, it too shrinks, leaving the fitting loose. You can avoid this problem with the push-tenon design (which is used in most fine pipes) by cleaning the pipe after a smoke with the stem in and only removing the stem for a thorough cleaning after a day or two of drying in the rack.

Do not leave a cleaner in the shank as the pipe is drying because it will prevent a normal air flow from drying the shank. If a pipe stem becomes loose, the smoker should take it to a good pipemaker, who usually will be able to swell the tenon, returning the pipe to its proper condition.

Problem: The stem is too tight or frozen in place. Or the stem does not fit flush to the end of the shank.

Solution: These problems are caused by the same things that cause a shank to split or a stem to loosen. The smoker with either of these difficulties is lucky that the damage is not more severe.

If a stem is too tight or frozen, one must be careful to avoid splitting the shank or snapping the stem. First, let the pipe sit for several days or weeks until it is thoroughly dry. At this time you should be able to remove the stem as the swollen wood will have con-

Personal character of "Chair with Pipe," by Vincent Van Gogh, reflects the intimacy with which these objects are associated. In this painting, pipe and pouch are mementos of artist's father.

233

tracted. If the fitting does not loosen naturally, take or send your pipe to a tobacconist and let him repair it. With a push-tenon type of stem these problems generally result from prolonged misuse. If the pipe is allowed to rest properly and is not oversmoked, the smoker occasionally can pull the stem out after smoking without causing any damage. Only when a pipe is oversmoked and full of moisture and tars do problems such as these occur. It is wise, nevertheless, to refrain from habitually removing the stem directly after smoking.

If the stem does not fit tightly against the end of the shank, it may be due to a build-up of tars in the end of the shank which will not allow the tenon to seat properly. This looseness could also be caused by pulling the stem out too often and neglecting to clean the shank properly. A pipe in this condition is a perfect target for easy breakage because the stem is not well supported and this lack of support weakens the fitting.

Problem: Your curved stem has straightened.
Solution: This generally happens when one leaves a pipe in the sun for a long time (for instance, on the dashboard of a closed car parked in the sun). All vulcanite stems originally are straight. After they are fitted to the pipe they are heated and bent. When exposed to extreme heat, they straighten to their original molded shape.

If this happens, remove the stem from the pipe and slowly heat it over a low flame (such as provided by an alcohol lamp), moving it back and forth slowly, keeping it above the flame. When it becomes pliable, hold it in a towel and press it gently back into the proper curve. Hold it in this position for a minute or so, then put it under a faucet and let cold water run over it.

Problem: The stem is broken.
Solution: A good tobacco shop should be able to replace a broken stem at a reasonable price. Don't ask for an exchange as breaks of this type are not caused by defects. To avoid breakage, smoke sturdy pipes when you are active and don't carry your pipes in your pants or shirt pocket. Most important, do not pound your pipe out while holding it at the stem. Pipes with narrow shanks are just not as durable as hammers.

Problem: It is difficult or impossible to push a cleaner through a bent stem.
Solution: The channels of the bit and shank may be offset in a pipe with a bent stem, thus causing a cleaner to hang up. Manufacturers of better pipes drill a trough that guides the cleaner to the shank portion of the channel as it comes through the stem. Unfortunately this is not done to most pipes. However, the cleaner will often go on through if you push it through the stem gently until it stops, and then give it a quarter or half turn. If this does not work, you will have to remove the stem to clean the pipe. However, remember to let the pipe cool and dry out first.

Picture Credits·

PART I

6: NS. 10-11: Old Museum Village of Smith's Clove/AS. 13-14: NYPL. 15: DE/NS. 17-19: NYPL. 22: Tobacco Institute (top), NYPL (bottom l.), WC (bottom center), Museum of the American Indian (bottom r.). 23-25: NYPL. 26-27: WC. 28: John J. Adler (top), Brooklyn Museum (center), Museum of the American Indian (bottom). 31: John J. Adler (top), Smithsonian Institution (center), Walters Art Gallery (bottom). 32-36: NYPL. 38: NYPL/Prints Division (top), Cooper-Hewitt Museum of Decorative Arts and Design, Smithsonian Institution (bottom). 39: Prado Museum.

PART II

42-43: Collection of Ambassador and Mrs. J. William Middendorf, II, N.Y. 45: NYPL. 46-47: Worcester Art Museum. 48: WC. 49: AM/NS. 50-51: NYPL. 52-53: Arno Hammacher. 54: Detroit Institute of Arts (top), WC (bottom). 55: DE/NS. 57: AM/NS. 58: Royal Copenhagen/AS. 60: National Collection of Fine Arts. 61: Missouri Meerschaum Co., Washington, Mo./AS. 62: AM/NS. 63: Private collection. 64: DE/NS. 66: Louvre, Paris. 68: NYPL. 69: PS. 71: Nelson Gallery-Atkins Museum, Kansas City, Mo. 72: Royal Museum of Fine Arts, Copenhagen. 74-75: St. Louis Art Museum. 77-80: VM. 82-84: DE/NS. 85: VM. 86-87: Museum of Fine Arts, Springfield, Mass. 88-89: DE/NS. 90: WC. 91: VM (top), WC (bottom). 92: VM. 93: Allen Memorial Art Museum. 96-100: NS. 103: Wilke Pipe Shop/AS. 105: AM/NS. 106-107: VM. 108: AM/NS. 109: DE/NS. 110: Hermitage Museum. 111: AM/NS. 112: DE/NS. 114: AM/NS (l.), Cooper-Hewitt Museum of Decorative Arts and Design (r.). 115: Cleveland Museum of Art, Mr. and Mrs. William H. Marlatt Fund. 116: Wilke Pipe Shop/AS. 117: Connoisseur Pipe Shop, Ltd. 119-122: Arlington Briar Corp., Brooklyn, N.Y./NS. 124: Wilke Pipe Shop. 126-129: Savinelli Pipes, Inc./AS. 132-133: Lane, Ltd./AS. 136: All pipes from Wally Frank, Ltd., except two briars on r. from A.

Oppenheimer & Co./AS.

PART III

138-139: RM. 141: PS. 142-145: RM. 146: American Brands Co. 148-152: RM. 155: NYPL. 157: NYPL. 158: CP. 159-160: NYPL. 163: CP. 164-165: Niemeyer Nederlands Tabacologisch Museum. 166: NYPL. 167: North Carolina Museum of Art, Raleigh, N. Carolina. 169: Rijksmuseum, Amsterdam. 170: DE/NS. 171: PS. 172-173: Musée des Beaux Arts de la Ville de Liége. 174-175: Musées Royaux des Beaux-Arts. 176: Old Museum Village of Smith's Clove/AS. 180: CP. 181: NYPL. 182: Brown Brothers. 184: Tobacco and Textile Museum, Danville, Virginia. 185: CP. 186: VM. 187: Tobacco and Textile Museum. 190: Clockwise from Indian at r.: Smithsonian Institution; Abby Aldrich Rockefeller Folk Art Collection, Colonial Williamsburg; Maryland Historical Society; New-York Historical Society; Abby Aldrich Rockefeller Folk Art Collection, Colonial Williamsburg. 191: New-York Historical Society (l.), Shelburne Museum (c.), Virginia Museum of Fine Arts (r.). 192: CP. 194: Collections of Greenfield Museum and The Henry Ford Museum. 195: DE/NS. 198-201: AS.

PART IV

204-205: NYPL/Prints Division. 206: NYPL. 208: Metropolitan Museum of Art. 211: Kröller-Müller Museum. 212: PS (top), Niemeyer Nederlands Tabacologisch Museum (bottom). 213: PS. 214: Niemeyer Nederlands Tabacologisch Museum (top & center), H. F. and P. H. F. Reemtsma (bottom). 216: National Maritime Museum, Greenwich, England. 218-219: NYPL. 220: Corcoran Gallery of Art. 222: Tobacco and Textile Museum. 223: Library of Congress (l.), Niemeyer Nederlands Tabacologisch Museum. 224: DE/NS. 226: Tobacco and Textile Museum. 227: American Brands Co. 228: Old Museum Village of Smith's Clove/AS. 231: Hermitage Museum. 232: Tate Gallery, London.

235

Index

References to pipe and tobacco illustrations in italics

236